AF469434

The Narrow Line

THE NARROW LINE

An Anatomy of Professional Cricket

GEOFF COOK and NEVILLE SCOTT

The Kingswood Press

In memory of Des

First published in Great Britain in 1991
by The Kingswood Press
an imprint of Methuen London
Michelin House, 81 Fulham Road, London sw3 6rb

Copyright © 1991 Geoff Cook and Neville Scott

A CIP catalogue record for this book
is available from the British Library
isbn 0 413 65550 4

Typeset in 12 on 13½pt Linotron Baskerville
by Hewer Text Composition Services, Edinburgh
Printed in Great Britain
by Mackays of Chatham plc, Chatham, Kent

Contents

Acknowledgements

Our thanks are due to the *Northampton Chronicle & Echo*, especially librarian Christine Cole, for assistance with photographs; to Patrick Eagar for the front jacket illustration; and to Bob Sedgwick for the author photograph.

Part of the argument in chapter nine draws upon ideas first developed in an article in the *Cricketer* in 1988. Our thanks to that magazine for permission to re-examine the material here.

We must acknowledge also the proof reading and editorial assistance of Jacqueline Blair. First drafts of various sections of this book were kindly read by Nick Cook, Stephen Coverdale, Tim Curtis, Alan Fordham and Jim Watts. Their expressions of disagreement and even incomprehension were quite as helpful as their words of encouragement! Needless to say, the opinions, and faults, which remain are entirely those of the authors.

Many of the examples which support the thrust of our arguments are taken from over twenty years of Northamptonshire cricket. Our recognition must be extended to all the players who have represented the county in that time and, not least, to those contemporary players who have put up with Neville Scott's obscure lines of questioning over the last three seasons.

Foreword *by Mike Brearley*

This is an unusual cricket book. It has few anecdotes or match descriptions; it is self-effacing and does not rely on the heroics of star players. It offers instead a detailed, reflective and intricate analysis of the life of a professional cricketer and his team in England today. Unlike most sports books this one takes seriously questions about the individual and the group, about self-discipline and imposed discipline, about team morale and self-fulfilment. It sees the achievements of the individual, and his experience within the team, not as simple, linear events but as multi-dimensional, embedded in contexts. The writers do not jib at the attempt to describe these complexities; like the reflective, developing cricketer they present to us, they seek a personal philosophy of the game, of its values and its potential. They paint a portrait of a profession, from inside and outside. Collaborators from either side of the boundary, Geoff Cook and Neville Scott write as lovers of this strange game, a game that can last almost a week and yet be hardly nearer a decisive result at the end than at the beginning.

I will give you a taste of just one of the many themes explored in their pages; of 'the . . . complex interrogation of his character' which the developing cricketer needs to make if he is to fulfil his talent, not only in terms of personal tallies, but also in terms of gaining the total respect of his colleagues. The authors recognise three phases in this process which I may paraphrase as childhood, adolescence and adulthood. Contrary to popular belief, the first-team infant and small child is encouraged and supported unless he shows unacceptable failures of attitude, like tantrums or crude selfishness. The need for advice is noted but so too is the essential fact that each toddler has to take his own first steps. 'A team can only relate to the character which is allowed to reveal itself.' That emerging character may, of course, be daunted by powerful personalities or stifled by their (actual or imagined) patronising of his efforts. Like the real baby, he enters an environment – committee, captain, coach, colleagues, club ethos – which may hold him and facilitate his developments, or it may smother his growth.

In the second stage – adolescence, perhaps – there are growing expectations. A self-examination is now called for, and it is demanded that advice be taken in and thought about. Standards both from outside the player and within him become more exacting and realistic. Here the authors stress the need, as they see it, for a thorough and honest appraisal of one's position in the club and in the team, of one's strengths and weaknesses, and also of one's commitment to the career. Without this, they argue, a player is unlikely to mature fully. They also describe the need to grow up within the nexus of the team, finding one's own way to express oneself in the context of team needs and mores. Some latitude of behaviour and standards is allowed, especially for those whose talents have been tried and tested; the younger player has yet to convince his team-mates that his aberrations of technique, preparation and behaviour are worth tolerating.

The final stage? Well, all you need to do is read on. Psychologically, socially, tactically, this book will stimulate you to think, debate and disagree: but usually to agree. For example, the discussion on pitches in chapter four is the most complete that I have read, embracing in a sophisticated yet thoroughly common-sense way both the fact that county cricket is a worthwhile end in itself (and in this pitches are vital) and the fact that it needs to be a breeding-ground for Test cricket.

The authors rightly remind us of the need to control primitive animosities in the interests of the task. Such control is indeed a feature of maturation, both in individuals and in teams. It is also perhaps the case, though, that real maturity permits the more primitive feelings to be expressed (up to a point) *without* demolishing the adult personality or the structures of a group. I have described some of the Middlesex teams in which I played as collections of atoms in constant lively collision with each other, an interaction which, though sometimes uncomfortable, did not preclude cohesive action where it counted. So I

should probably not have been surprised to read here of the
'fractious cricketers' and the 'palpable collective disharmony'
of the Middlesex dressing-room of the early 1980s. Geoff Cook
and Neville Scott remind me that it all might have been a bit
more peaceful!

Introduction

On 15 July 1971 I was in Southport watching the second day of Lancashire's match against Northamptonshire, the side I had supported for as long as I had followed the game. I slept under canvas in a village outside the town having hitch-hiked across the Pennines from Leeds, the venue for the last Test. The following day the 19-year-old Geoff Cook, making his third county appearance, would record his maiden first-class 50. But by this time, tent pulled up, I was back on the road, appalled at the disdainful ease with which Jack Bond and David Hughes had mauled my county the previous afternoon as they established near-certain victory. What I *had* witnessed in fact, as 'we' were skittled out before lunch, was Geoff Cook's maiden first-class duck. In all conscience, I cannot pretend to remember this.

Some astounding things happen in life. The youth, fresh from his O-levels, could little know, as he thumbed a lift on the East Lancs. Road, that seventeen years later he would be commentating on Cook each day and interviewing him once a fortnight. Far less that they would go on to write a book together.

As cricket books have proliferated in the last few years, there has been much comment about ghosted reminiscence. This is not a work of biography or autobiography; it seeks to be one of dispassionate analysis, and it is a collaborative venture. It may be of interest to offer a brief note on the mechanics of its authorship.

The basis of each save the last two of the nine chapters was a lengthy taping session preceded by pages of dense, handwritten notes. Once we had decided which areas would have to be covered in any serious review of professional cricket, we set aside a series of afternoons for discussion. In advance of these, I prepared detailed outlines of the questions I thought we needed to address, and Geoff would then work on these for about a week, pursuing certain points on paper and adding further themes of his own. In this way we hoped to ensure a systematic approach to the subject before us. Our discussions over the winter following Geoff Cook's retirement from Northamptonshire in 1990 confirmed a close similarity of outlook. In some senses, perhaps, this is not entirely to the good. It had been our intention, should disagreement arise, to place both positions forward, possibly even side by side.

The bulk of the book is divided evenly between what could be termed very loosely theory and practice. Such compartmentalism can never be exact because the factors which influence a professional cricketer are only really relevant as they are revealed in performance. But we do not fully take the field until chapter four. Prior to that we are, respectively, in the dressing-room, at the drawing-board and within the debates of a club's committees. Thereafter we consider the three types of professional cricket in turn. The most detailed chapter here, and the core of the book, is unashamedly that discussing the County Championship, still the heart of England's professional game. The seventh chapter returns us, rather tentatively, to the cricketer himself, the individual who must come to terms with a complex sport and the even more complex interrogation of his character that it entails.

In the middle of the book's preparation, Durham acceded to first-class status and Geoff to the post of that county's Director of Cricket. Indeed, our taped discussion for the chapter on one-day cricket took place at Lord's while in a nearby room the TCCB finalised the draft of that historic announcement. To Geoff now falls, therefore, a dubious opportunity: to translate words into deeds, even as would-be junior professionals protest, 'That's not what it says in the book'!

Neville Scott, February 1991

ONE

The Making of a Professional Cricketer

'Show me the man and I'll tell you
the kind of cricketer he is.' DAVID STEELE

Nothing in cricket even begins to compare with the intense psychological rupture involved in moving from a county Second XI to the First XI. The transition is unique, the gulf wider by far than that between good club cricket and representative youth cricket, colts cricket and Second XI cricket, or even county cricket and Test cricket. Nothing can adequately prepare the newcomer for the competitive bite that is immediately tangible in a first-team dressing-room. When play begins, some of its unfolding patterns will be familiar and consoling. But the attitude of the players involved will remain fundamentally different from anything he has experienced before.

In an English cricket season about 350 professionals take to the first-class field. Of these, perhaps 250 at most will have had significant experience of the game's requirements and have found their way towards a working assessment of how these can best be met. At no stage in his development will an aspiring professional, bidding to join this committed few, have encountered such concentrated determination to succeed. The venues for Second XI cricket are often club grounds whose inferior pitches prompt an unconscious lowering of standards; even professionals with several years at the top behind them will rarely perform to their fullest in these arenas. Five wickets for the Second XI, or a century scored in adversity, will be acknowledged and applauded by the members of a county squad. Not for a moment, however, will they suggest that such feats equal even the more minor triumphs at the higher level. Indeed, it is widely accepted that real talent will actually begin to decline if its opportunity is restricted to the Second XI for too long.

These are problems which clubs have increasingly begun to address. Second XI matches are now played under the same technical conditions as Championship matches, their limited-over games mirror the general format of the senior knock-out competitions and better playing surfaces are continually encouraged. Where once the captaincy of the Second XI was something of a reward for a long-serving professional, with or without regard to his aptitude as coach and teacher, appointments are now made with considerable care. The Second XI captain is asked to find ways of fostering in his charges those attitudes of mind which might lessen the shock of genuinely competitive cricket. Yet cricket below the first-class level is so far short of the real thing that it cannot even approximately simulate its demands.

When speaking of differences in play, the differences they are most able to put into words, newcomers to the First XI make broadly similar observations. Bowlers comment that the errors which escape detection at the junior level are unfailingly punished by experienced batsmen who smell the chance of easy runs. For batsmen, the opportunities to score are severely constrained and so demand patience, extreme concentration and an element of improvisation. It is surprising how often the remark is made that the ball is hit with unexpected power by first-class cricketers; that is, in the field, it arrives with alarming speed.

These, however, are only tokens of the acute extent to which first-class cricket places its emphasis on confidence and the positive need to impose talent on unresolved events. As an experienced batsman upsets a newcomer's self-esteem by punishing error, so he hopes to induce further error. The more a beginner can be disturbed by his inability to score runs, the more likely he is to succumb to pressure and give his wicket away. Inexperience here compounds the problem; if certain situations have never before been confronted, it is difficult for a newcomer to assess whether he is coping badly or well. He will not know what represents an acceptable number of runs for a bowler to concede under the circumstances or, as a batsman, when exactly survival is more important than stroke-play.

These are weaknesses – both technical and psychological – which the opposition does its unremitting best to exploit. Part of Essex and England seamer John Lever's analysis of why

Keith Fletcher was such an excellent county captain was that he possessed an unrivalled ability to probe almost instantly into the flaws in a new batsman's character and technique. When Australia's Dennis Lillee came to Northamptonshire in 1988 almost all the batsmen he met on the county circuit were new to him. It was Lillee's belief that he had failed if, after only two or three overs, he had not worked out the way to get a batsman out. Once disclosed, these shortcomings will be passed on from player to player in the course of a season, and the apprentice's anxiety will grow ever more uncomfortable.

The newcomer's county colleagues, those already established in the dressing-room he enters, will have some appreciation of the difficulties he faces; to what degree can they assist – or, indeed, hinder – his path to self-realisation? There is probably a tendency, at least initially, to offer only the inanities of football management. Trite encouragements to 'play your own game' or 'go out and enjoy yourself' will usually have to suffice, and although this is clearly inadequate, it has to be accepted that captains and senior players will almost certainly be hampered by the fact that they know little of the man they find themselves trying to counsel. Their own playing commitments throughout the season provide few opportunities to watch a newcomer play or form any personal relationship with him.

For this reason, there is perhaps an argument for offering a set of modest guidelines. These might stress, for example, the need to remain unconcerned about slow scoring. Or a captain could acknowledge the kinds of feelings all cricketers naturally experience early in their careers. Setting targets suitable to the player's stage of development may also prove beneficial. When Young England batsman Neil Stanley gained a run of three Championship matches in the Northamptonshire side in 1989, he admitted that it would have been reassuring to hear captain Allan Lamb express some recognition of the different levels of expectation. In his pre-season team-talk Lamb had dwelt on the need to score a good half-century at least every second match, but Stanley felt that, as a 19-year-old, the more realistic goal of a substantial innings every third match would have inspired him with the confidence to deliver something of value to his team-mates.

The Narrow Line

At the same time there are very good reasons why advice and instruction at this early stage should be extremely tentative. A captain and a team can ultimately only relate to the character which is allowed to reveal itself, and the complex process by which a side will draw a newcomer into the coherence of the unit and grant him an identity with its own specific contribution to make, cannot be forced. In effect, the young player should be allowed to perform without additional pressure and be as self-expressive as possible so that his natural game can come through. If the newcomer is overburdened with his colleagues' versions of appropriate performance, the emergence of his own cricketing character will be all the more impeded.

There is no short cut to the establishment of the relationship between an individual and each of his fellows in a settled dressing-room. In this cricket is hardly unusual: any group requires time to discover the influence which a newcomer is gradually exerting. There is, however, one crucial difference. A professional cricket team has a painfully unambiguous purpose, to win cricket matches, and this purpose must be reflected both in the team's sense of direction on the field and in its dressing-room harmony.

As the young player attempts to come to grips with some of these facts for himself he will, for the most part, carry the genuine support and goodwill of his team-mates. The sincerity of this response is worth stressing. The impression probably still persists in the public mind, informed by stories of the atmosphere at the Oval in the 1950s or in the Yorkshire dressing-room of the 1960s, that cricket teams are uncharitable hosts beset by a stern preoccupation with status and seniority. The tale – apocryphal or not – that Geoff Boycott was deliberately run out early in his career by a fellow Yorkshire batsman because he was seen as a threat to that batsman's future has almost no contemporary resonance.

It is true that when a newcomer has performed reasonably well for a season or so certain professionals will begin to look at his progress in relation to their own position in the side. Semi-established cricketers, who are necessarily the most vulnerable, may then begin to nitpick in their assessment of the newcomer and lose both their objectivity and their readiness to make allowances for youth. This, however, will only become an issue of any real importance if it presents a deep threat to the balance of the team.

There is, then, a far greater probability of immediate integration into the dressing-room – and a far less pronounced obligation to defer at all times to one's betters – than was the case for a young player even twenty years ago. Since cricket now exists in a highly sponsored and commercially-conscious environment, it attaches great importance to success and does not wish to squander the asset of young talent. In this more mobile cricketing age, a potential star can invariably find a welcome elsewhere if he is made to feel unwelcome at 'home'.

Moreover, cricket seems to lend itself to collective participation and responsibility in the pursuit of success in a way that other games do not. It is hard to see how a rigid pattern could be imposed on cricketers by an outside strategist in the way that a football manager drills his players into conformity. Indeed, the increasing technical and administrative complexity of the 1990s, and an education system which seeks to foster decision-making and initiative, could hardly countenance those county regimes which allegedly once existed. The notion of the old amateur captain delivering orders which his professionals would then unquestioningly execute belongs to another era, not only of cricket, but of social history.

The reception offered to the newcomer, then, is essentially one of sincere welcome and encouragement. This will only markedly change, in the initial phase of a newcomer's career, if he begins to reveal facets of his character which go against the professional grain – displays of juvenile temper, for example, or inordinate selfishness, behaviour which is frowned upon by the traditions of the game. There is greater tolerance by far of playing error and technical frailty than of unacceptable conduct. The attitude of most averagely gifted professionals is that a cricketing 'apprenticeship' probably never ends, and therefore to find excessive early fault would be unfair. When defects of attitude are uncovered, however, respect is more rapidly eroded.

In spite of the fact that the passage into a county side is generally eased by colleagues, the experience can remain intimidating. When opening batsman Alan Fordham first regularly joined the ranks of Northamptonshire's senior eleven in 1988, the self-confidence of a degree from Durham University behind him, he nonetheless confessed to severe disorientation at sharing a dressing-room with men he had previously placed on pedestals. Young England cricketers Wayne Noon and Tony Penberthy admitted to being positively daunted by the presence of so powerful and imposing a personality as Allan Lamb in the same Northamptonshire side.

It is often the case that the very best of the established talents have difficulty relating to the uncertainties of newcomers, as a direct result of having themselves found the game so much easier. At the psychological level, the force of character which has enabled such players to flourish in Test cricket and put failure quickly behind them does not naturally invite an understanding of another's self-doubt. When Allan Lamb was appointed to the Northamptonshire captaincy in 1989 he confronted, possibly for the first time, elements of his own psychological make-up which had been nurtured in the unsophisticated culture of South Africa and so perhaps obstructed his ability to relate to others.

It is revealing to note the different ways in which a newcomer's insecurity can be expressed. For all-rounder Tony Penberthy there was a tendency to score 2 rather than 4, his stroke-play curbed by a fear of dismissal and the sense that he would thereby fall short of what was expected of him. For Wayne Noon, both captain and wicket-keeper on Young England's tour of Australia in 1989–90, the encouragement of his colleagues was found to be almost insulting. When congratulated by slip fielders for takes down the leg side which he himself regarded as regulation, he began to wonder whether the others believed he did not really know his job.

In his infancy, as it were, the newcomer will gain a lot of commendable support from established players; if an error can be isolated, or becomes the subject of implicit criticism, it will only cease to be forgiven if it is repeated time and again. By the second full year of his career, as his relationship with the team develops beyond general *bonhomie*, it will be expected that the newcomer should know better. The error will not usually be minutely analysed or outspokenly condemned; few captains pretend that professional cricket is at all an easy game. But quiet words of guidance are intended to be contemplated and taken in: it is expected that the newcomer will learn for himself. Here, the first-class game does not offer a compromise.

The young Geoff Cook, playing for Northamptonshire in the early 1970s under the captaincy of Jim Watts, was once dismissed by a spinner in a Sunday League match, caught on the long-on boundary. Cook's own feeling was that, since the shot was within a foot of carrying for 6, his downfall was largely unlucky. Watts made the quiet point that the circumstances had demanded pragmatic batting, not glory, and said, 'I thought you'd have been able to assess situations a bit better by now.' At this stage, Cook had been cast as a relatively dour batsman who should know his own limitations. Alan Tait, a more flamboyant opener at the start of an eight-year career with Northamptonshire and Gloucestershire which was to know only moderate success, scored a good 40 shortly afterwards before getting out with apparently equal irresponsibility. Watts inquired in the dressing-room where Tait was and went off to give what all expected to be a firm rebuke. In fact, he congratulated the youngster warmly, in the hope, no doubt, that this would give him greater confidence to examine the particular merits of his own individual game.

Given that the individual has received good advice from his coach and a reasonably compassionate welcome from the dressing-room, he becomes obliged to think for himself. In the winter nights of the off-season, whether in Britain or playing abroad, the cricketer must assess his own experiences. He needs to analyse for himself his position in the team, in the club and within the game itself. He needs to know why he is playing cricket and whether he has the dedication to continue doing so. Most important, he has to begin to understand the strengths and weaknesses in his own game and what these can be expected to contribute to the success of a team, given that his performance has no other context. It becomes imperative for every cricketer, whatever his level of natural ability, to establish a strategy for his own development over a period of at least two or three years. The extent of his self-fulfilment will largely depend on the speed with which he can do this and the rigour of his own analysis.

If such questions of attitude and commitment are ultimately addressed and resolved in solitude, there is still certain practical advice which can be passed on. Although young players should be allowed the freedom of expression to find where their talents lie, they must ensure that they do themselves justice, and the values they adopt and the methods of preparation they apply – whether for a single day's play, for a match or for a whole season – should denote a certain respect for their own ability. This entails, therefore, that they maintain their bodies in good shape, that they watch, learn, practise, listen, talk and sift out right and wrong influences. All preparation should be directed towards the capacity to pass through the dressing-room door and take the field in the best possible physical and emotional state. In short, the player should seek to let down neither himself nor his team.

Such neat maxims are altogether too facile, however, much easier offered than followed. The continuing problem for the individual cricketer is once again to know precisely what forms of preparation are applicable to himself, and standard routines of exercise and mental tuning, valuable though they often are in the creation of team unity, are no substitute for this knowledge. It is probably healthiest for an individual to develop a relationship with one given senior figure rather than to entertain so much advice as to lose direction. Many cricketers unconsciously cast a particular person in the role of confidant and even confessor, and it is in no sense necessary that this person should be a member of their team.

Chris and Robin Smith of Hampshire and England have long prospered because they have enjoyed a magnificent relationship with their father. Dennis Amiss, throughout his career with Warwickshire, turned time and again to the county's former England wicket-keeper, 'Tiger' Smith. Since 'Tiger' was not only in his 80s, but by then blind, it can be appreciated that Amiss was gaining something altogether more profound than advice on batting difficulties or the technical needs of one-day cricket. These practical elements are arguably nothing compared with the far more demanding problems of achieving self-awareness and finding a mode of coexistence with a group whose collective working harmony is the vital element in their success.

In view of the psychological and emotional complexity of the professional dressing-room, and of the game of cricket itself, there are many potential sources of conflict. It is difficult to find apposite analogies for the peculiar conditions under which first-class cricket is played in England. Where else do a given collection of people spend ten hours a day in each other's company for five and a half months at a time, release often coming for just two days in twenty? Which other group knows that, throughout such a period, it has an unavoidable purpose every time it assembles? Success or failure here is not restricted to the work-place; it is subject to the scrutiny of the millions who read the scorecards in their daily newspapers. Comparable stress might – only half-fancifully – be found in the conditions of penal servitude. It is not for melodramatic effect alone, perhaps, that cricket draws its imagery so heavily from the language of the battlefield.

Such metaphors, however, can never reflect the real place of emphasis in cricket: on the individual. Cricketers are invariably denied the luxury of mere obedience; only rarely do they receive simple commands and equally rarely, therefore, can they evade the burden of personal responsibility. Given the need for an individual to work out the contribution of his strengths and weaknesses to the common aim of team success, one obvious source of conflict is the difference between the player's assessment of his role and that which the balance of the side has assigned him.

This is a problem which frequently arises with fast bowlers. Bowlers are often more sensitive than batsmen in that their role is physically harder and their reliance on team-mates, to stop runs and take catches, is so much more evident. If a player's perception of himself is as a front-line wicket-taker, he may believe that he should bowl with a hard ball and the wind behind him, and he may expect that his devotion to finding deliveries good enough to remove top-order batsmen should grant him a certain licence to concede runs. However, if the club decides that, due to natural aptitude or the presence of better qualified strike bowlers in the squad, he is more suited to containment, the potential for discord is clear. The need is for the club to remain sensitive to the individual's insecurity and pride, and yet be quite steely in setting out the role it envisages and insists upon – the iron fist in the velvet glove. The problem may be exacerbated by the fact that the bowler, especially when young and inexperienced, has not been party to the formulation of game plans which have ascribed him the task he resents. Professional cricketers are always ready to express their admiration for the ability to keep things tight and 'hold an end', but the phrases they use for the player – at best the 'stock bowler', at worst the 'donkey' – are hardly flattering.

Ideally there are three separate factors which will come together. The captain and coach will be entirely fair to the bowler's abilities in determining the part he should play, and they will outline his role with honesty; the senior players will back the bowler at all times in fulfilling this role; and the individual's realistic assessment of his own aptitudes will lead him to concede the merits of the case which has been made. In actuality, of course, genuine differences of perception can endure. A compromise may be reached in an agreement to give the bowler all available scope (bringing him on as soon as match conditions allow, granting him a more attacking role if a wicket is taken), but if the disagreement remains fundamental there is no simple solution. At Northampton the problem was confronted with the young, very gifted and typically highly-strung fast bowler, Mark Robinson. A fully satisfactory conclusion was never found, and Robinson returned to his native Yorkshire in 1991, attracted by the prospect of the new ball.

A player who seriously deludes himself throughout his career will ultimately never fulfil his potential. Fast bowlers more than any other cricketers tend to back their own judgements to the point of changing clubs, and there are at least ten who, in recent seasons, have sought success elsewhere. Although it is rarely the case that they have departed with any deep animosity, or even solely because they felt they were being inappropriately handled, it is equally unusual for their careers to take a sudden turn for the better.

A suitable metaphor for the way in which a dressing-room orders itself and pursues its working harmony may well be that of a beam upon which the player has to walk. The beam defines the limits of acceptable conduct and the degree of licence which can be afforded. Some players, perhaps even to their own detriment, will never stray very far from the middle of the beam throughout their careers; they will seek a modest, sober conformity with what they consider to be solid professional standards. Others will walk more consistently towards the edge and risk the ignominy of very public falls from grace.

The bounds which the beam sets can only relate to the game itself. A player's private life and leisure time is his own affair; it is not required of a professional that he should like all his team-mates, simply that he should be able to play with them for the good of the side. Therefore it is only when traits of character reveal themselves harmfully on the field, perhaps in terms of disinterestedness or indiscretion, that reproach is in order. Equally, if elements of a player's outside life or psychological make-up intrude disruptively into the dressing-room, they may then be legitimately questioned. 'Working harmony', for which might sometimes as truthfully be substituted 'controlled animosity', is precisely what the term implies: a balance designed for work, not for life. Genuine friendship between particular players may well enhance their enjoyment of a match, but the readiness of a fielder to work hard for a bowler, or of a batsman to support his partner, clearly cannot depend on personal respect; such obligations must be undertaken as part of the professional outlook.

Everybody will be permitted to slip from the beam occasionally. Cricketers recognise that it is exceptionally difficult to maintain a high level of concentration and commitment for the length of an arduous season, and loss of form in particular will invite its own degrees of empathy. The misery and strain of that experience is understood to induce uncharacteristic lapses: a batsman may play an inappropriate shot in his desperation for runs, or a bowler may try too hard and lose control. Moreover, more talented players are allowed to fall from the beam a little more spectacularly than others and will almost certainly be more easily forgiven.

On the face of it, this seems wholly unjust and potentially harmful to team spirit. In practice, however, players do concede that the rules do not apply uniformly across the board. They are aware that success in cricket rests heavily on creative expression: the same confidence and ability which enable a cricketer to turn a match almost on his own will sometimes lead to overambition or errors of judgement. Cricketers are frequently more fair in their assessment of this than spectators. Championship success relies heavily on the ability to score runs and to improvise in unfavourable circumstances, and the capacity of Wayne Larkins to do this for Northamptonshire has often manufactured outrageous advantage out of nothing, an opportunism all the more admirable for the fact that it courts failure. Yet, if Larkins falls early in his innings to an ostensibly rash stroke, the muttering of complaint from the crowd all too readily overlooks his past triumphs.

A further pertinent example is provided by the player who returns to his county from duty with England. The captain and the team should be prepared to accept that anyone who is deeply involved in a Test series will need to relax; since county cricket continues virtually without a rest, the only place where he will be able to relax is on the field. Such special dispensation cannot last too long, however, and after a reasonable period a captain will once more demand absolute and evident commitment to county success, especially if the relaxation has manifested itself in a loose shot or inadequate zest with the ball. Yet this can work both ways: a relaxed way of playing in difficult circumstances can provide colleagues with confidence and inspiration, and a man of Test calibre, hardened in international cricket, can pass on an air of control and assurance which a tense dressing-room will welcome. The divide between frivolity and confidence is thin.

This example makes an important point regarding the subtle ways in which particular attitudes influence team performance. The beam is broader for certain players because a pedantic application of blanket rules does not take into account the actual means by which strong individuals forge their collective identity, nor how diverse attributes bring about the well-rounded ability of the whole. There are occasions, certainly, when everything can go wrong with a side, when individual deficiencies in attitude communicate themselves to the collective and players allow general failure to justify their own personal negligence.

The better sides are those that sense this immediately, avoid recrimination and return to the beam most quickly.

It should not be forgotten that those who come together in a first-team dressing-room are all highly proficient at their chosen game and have considerable insight into the demands it makes and into how those demands may be shirked. It is sometimes argued that the high quality of English umpiring comes from the fact that most officials are ex-professionals who thus know very well the tricks of their former trade. In a similar way, it is difficult for a player to conceal from his team-mates any sustained irresponsibility, while each player's knowledge of the game's demands dictates a degree of qualified leniency with talent.

This again helps explain the apparent inconsistency between levels of tolerance granted to different players. A professional will often say of a fellow-cricketer that, 'You cannot argue with his record', and performance does indeed convey a great deal. Debate outside the game will not always concede the point so readily and will indeed argue with a man's record at considerable length, concentrating rather on alleged technical defects which have not in fact prevented the cricketer from taking hundreds of first-class wickets or scoring three centuries every season. A senior player is far more likely to stress the relative value of statistics to team performance in particular circumstances, but a young batsman, say, will not take lightly a senior's proven capability since he knows too well how difficult it is to score runs. A young player will often defer to standards appropriate to his own style and role. Thus Neil Stanley at Northampton, as a potentially powerful stroke-making batsman, has the highest regard for Wayne Larkins. The real test for Stanley will be to emulate not Larkins's methods, but his results, and here is the relevance of the beam: Larkins can be permitted his approach to batting because it has so often benefited the side, but those who wish to play like that will only ultimately be indulged if their contribution is similarly productive.

The largely unspoken bounds which are set for a dressing-room are defined by three processes. Most essentially, by the player's own careful consideration of what he believes appropriate to himself, a matter involving rigorous self-assessment;

by a captain's sensitive handling of individual characteristics and abilities in relation to the balance of the group; and, far more rarely, by the group's own assertion of what is acceptable in order to highlight transgression all the more glaringly and thereby impose their collective sanction.

By the time the newcomer has been in the side for two seasons, at the age of perhaps 22 or 23, he will be expected to provide significant and consistent contributions. He will now begin the process of becoming recognised in his own right, a known and respected quantity, and at grounds around the country supporters and players will identify him by name as they anticipate the visit of his team. The extent of this continuing growth of the player will owe much to the stability of his environment, as reflected in the attitude not only of the captain, but of the senior players around him.

The role of the senior player is vital. For a captain to give shape to his side he needs at least the acquiescence of his peers, and ideally their active co-operation in demonstrating what is required. There are two obvious reasons why this should not always be granted. There may be a deep-seated grudge held against the captain by the senior player, who may feel that he could do a better job and takes it as a slur that the club has passed him over. Alternatively the senior player may be so engrossed in his own performances that he does not have time to cultivate a global view. The full assistance of good senior players is invaluable in the captain's attempts at forging a working harmony, but equally potent is their capacity to undermine his plans by offering an alternative focus for the junior professionals. It is for this reason, perhaps, that so many counties are now turning to team managers, a development which has often merely side-stepped the problem, not resolved it.

Surrey surprised many people in 1986 by releasing Alan Butcher, but it was still thought short-sighted of Glamorgan that they should take up his registration. Butcher, however, came to a squad which contained only Rodney Ontong and John Hopkins over the age of 30, and was led by the recently appointed Hugh Morris, himself just 23. Hopkins stood on the verge of retirement and, though obviously unforeseen, Ontong was to be sadly injured in an accident a year later and he left the following season. Rejuvenation at Glamorgan is a relative matter, but the club's appreciable improvement during 1990, attributed in the main to the arrival of Viv Richards, owed much in fact to the fruits of Butcher's four-year influence. His effect was as significant in his first two seasons as in the next when Morris handed over the leadership because it had upset his batting. Glamorgan shrewdly recognised the benefit of an old hand in a young dressing-room, and inexperienced players quietly profited from Butcher's mature presence.

A very strange imbalance existed in the Northamptonshire camp through the 1990 season which saw four highly experienced players in the age range 33–37 (Nick Cook, Lamb, Larkins and Richard Williams) and five others in the range 25–28 (Rob Bailey, David Capel, Fordham, Alan Walker and Duncan Wild). The only two intermediaries, Nigel Felton and Greg Thomas, had both arrived the year before and were still to an extent establishing themselves in the dressing-room. The oddity of this circumstance was reflected in the fact that Northamptonshire had seen four benefit seasons in the five years to 1989, but were due to grant no more until 1995 – an unusual piece of discontinuity. It may well be that the two groups had become unknowingly separated in terms of the generation of common ideas and attitudes. The balance became unavoidably upset and there developed an unfair tendency for the one group to claim that the other lacked awareness and for the young contingent to feel excluded from authority. Interestingly enough, without it ever reflecting a conscious policy, Northamptonshire found themselves signing, or attempting to sign, four players in two years (1988–90) who bridged precisely this generation gap.

If we can say that counties will usually have in their first-team squads professionals between the ages of 22 and 37 (a few will force selection earlier, while some will remain in the side longer), then we are speaking of a span of some sixteen playing ages. As this will also be the approximate number of cricketers making a significant number of appearances for a county in any given season (in 1990 all but five counties had fifteen or more players who were employed in over a quarter of their Championship fixtures), then a rough rule of thumb might be that one new player will join each county's ranks every season. This would certainly indicate a healthy and continuous production of talent, and may also represent the best blend for the transmission of correct professional values through a squad. A great many reasons can be adduced for the pace-setting records of Essex and Middlesex over the last fifteen or so seasons, but it is not coincidental that both clubs have had almost exactly this spread of experience in their front-line strength.

Within this squad there will be two or three senior players to whom the captain looks not only for consistent runs and wickets, but for dressing-room support. If ability here is not allied to a due sense of responsibility there is a real danger of significant disquiet. Whatever flexibility is conveyed in the idea of the beam, this is not a problem to which the captain can turn a blind eye for too long. He must monitor the relationship between seniors and others very carefully and decide for himself when the time is right for intervention. It may be that the matter needs to be raised every three matches; it may only need to be aired after three months in mid-season. But the influence of senior attitudes on the working harmony is critical.

The next stage for the player who is no longer a newcomer will be to strike particular relationships with those of a similar outlook to himself. Dressing-rooms – even knocking-up periods before play – often feature groups of two or three people who are clearly most comfortable in each other's company, and this may then extend to a close and long-term friendship which has an evident bearing on their play. At Northampton, Alan Fordham and Nigel Felton examined this at length in a fascinating interview which revealed how an understanding of each other's philosophy of the game, and indeed of life, contributed to the success of what in 1990 was an unexpectedly productive opening partnership. Each, for example, had listened independently to a tape on the psychology of batting and, having discussed it on a long journey between fixtures, found that they agreed on what they considered to be its most worthwhile points. Knowing what the other was trying to express or do in his cricket enabled them to assist each other more perceptively. In a key 60-over fixture before a capacity crowd, their ability to exchange jokes about their nervousness at the crease, jokes which drew on comedy routines they knew each other to enjoy, enabled them to admit to their apprehension and, to a degree, dispel it in doing so.

Felton and Fordham are rather unusual because, perhaps a little surprisingly, two cricketers of the same age who are direct peers or have a similar standing in the game often find it most difficult to get on. This stems not only from the fact that the progress which they make in their respective careers will invariably be compared, but probably also from the fact that they feel that their private anxieties are apparent to the other. They will often be adept at hiding this resentment, and cricketers in general become very good at forming a veneer which prevents personal ill feeling jeopardising team performance. This will rarely be evident from the outside, and, indeed, team-mates may only realise that the veneer exists from the absence of warmth at various times. When two distanced players are exposed to each other's company – while batting together, for example, or fielding close to each other – it may be the averting of the eye rather than the exchange of glances which is revealing. Their very lack of conversation and mutual congratulation will speak loudly.

Only occasionally will this veneer crack, and then usually in times of strain on the field. The effect can, however, become cumulative. If pressure produces open rancour in a team it feeds longstanding antipathies and makes it more likely that similar periods of stress in the future will see the conflict reappear. Over the course of a season this need not affect results, but when a team repeatedly fails to control its emotions it will begin to dread close finishes, since anxiety at such key moments will, in the long term, be fatal.

More often than not, the underlying reason for a side's inability to translate the undisputed prowess of its individuals into collective success will be found in what press rumour usually labels 'a discontented dressing-room'. Contrary to what is perhaps imagined, this does not usually mean that the dressing-room is overendowed with unsavoury characters, but that the everyday veneer has splintered beyond repair. Consistent success does not accompany fractious cricketers, and the only exception in recent times to prove the rule might be the Middlesex dressing-room of the early 1980s. The fact that Middlesex did pull together despite individual eccentricities and palpable collective disharmony is a tribute to captain Mike Brearley. It also indicates, perhaps, just how cussed extremely good players can be in denying their enemies a reason to criticise them.

Part of the problem is that cricket requires such individual effort that self-made professionals can be reluctant to take on the additional burden of analysing their team. The professional game's emphasis on self-development does not naturally encourage group skills. Although clubs now seem prepared to commit considerable resources to the nurturing of talent from the age of 14 through to the first team, very few give any great thought to a player's social and emotional growth thereafter.

To what, it may be asked, is this growth directed; is there a definition, in the final analysis, of what constitutes a complete professional career? In personal terms, a county professional clearly aspires to Test selection and, more than that, to an evident record of achievement for his country. Few can realistically hope to attain that, however, and most cricketers concede as much. When pressed to offer an assessment of an opponent they genuinely admire, it is noticeable how often the shorthand of the circuit leads to almost identical formulations. 'X is a true professional', they say, or 'it was the kind of professional performance you always expect from X'. This will be true even when 'X' represents characters as diverse as, for example, Phil Carrick, Neil Foster and Desmond Haynes.

Professionalism here is defined as both the ability of a player to recognise what is required in any given situation and, more important, a readiness to devote himself unselfishly to the fulfilment of these requirements. This will be true whether the situation in question is the critical five overs which turn a match, or the five hours in which a lost cause is retrieved or a winning position is crafted. For most players, then, the compliment indicates an uncommon combination of cricketing intelligence, talent and especially attitude which exists in the man who will always commit himself to his side's success. There is a degree of acceptance among professionals that some are simply better at assessing the needs of a circumstance than others, and that some talents are inadequate to specific demands.

What will never be condoned is failure through self-interest or lack of attention.

This respect for professionalism is perhaps all the more heightened precisely because any inclination towards selfishness, resignation or withdrawal can be better masked in cricket than in most other sports. The batsman who gets out having scored 50 to avoid further physical punishment and mental strain, or the bowler who allows minor injury to persuade him he can be excused hard labour, will hardly ever be detected from the boundary. The 'true professional', in short, measures himself by his and his team-mates' own high and unforgiving standards.

It is, however, far easier to live by these good, professional codes if your county can be trusted to understand the game. In this sense success on the field is determined by the wider club outlook and philosophy, not purely by the quality of its players. The professional is made in a given context and, if he is to maintain unfailingly the requisite standards, the need for him to believe in the fairness of his employers is probably absolute.

There are millions of people who follow cricket through the newspapers and scrutinise the end-of-season averages. Though most would claim to accept that these mean little, they have unquestionably affected careers. Forty runs scored in ten overs at the crease to set up an early declaration are known by players to mean more than 80 slower runs which leave insufficient time to force victory. Too many good, middle-order batsmen have missed Test recognition because averages fail to reflect this. Yet if it is feared that a county committee will also misread performance, there will be a real disincentive to constant team play.

The real flaws in a professional's make-up, flaws which will assume truly threatening proportions in the dressing-room, are not in fact at all likely to be picked up by the outsider, but will be betrayed in apparently minor aspects of play. The onlooker will not usually realise, for example, when a batsman is manipulating the strike by pushing for singles so that he avoids his share of unpleasant bowling or helps himself to easy runs from weak bowling. Many people applaud a senior batsman's efforts to shield a tail-ender, but far fewer will appreciate when no such effort is realistically being made. Similarly, what will be noted approvingly as fine running between the wickets will never quite capture the extent to which this is a positive reflection of a batsman's goodwill, his ever-alert readiness to devote energy to a colleague's cause. Although a bowler may gain the warm affection of the crowd for completing over after over into a howling gale, nobody will know that perhaps each of his faster colleagues in turn has insistently refused the role.

The notoriety of Phillippe Edmonds only eventually became public when some explanation was finally required for his continuing omission from England sides. Edmonds was not taken abroad by England for five successive winters, despite being consistently the country's best slow left-armer and despite playing in two Test series at home in that time. Nobody doubted his passionate commitment to success on the field; it was his relationship with team-mates which was problematic. When it became known that England captain Bob Willis considered him so difficult to handle he refused to have him on tour, spectators finally became aware of conflicts that their own eyes had never revealed. Even regulars at Lord's who were party to the Middlesex gossip had only infrequently seen any evidence at all to explain why Mike Brearley should once, very famously, have dismissed Edmonds from the field.

A variant of the David Steele aphorism with which the chapter began might be heard in such dressing-room laments as 'if only we had eleven Alan Walkers, we'd be a much better team'. Walker, another of the 'true professionals', dedicates himself to Northamptonshire so completely, as seamer, fielder and limited left-hand tail-ender, that it can sometimes be to his disadvantage. Showing evident disgust with himself on occasion for producing a bad ball, he in fact surrenders some of the initiative to the opposing batsman who draws strength from Walker's dejection. It is easy to sympathise with the view the above sentiment implies, but in the last analysis it is not altogether true. For consistent success a county needs to ally the utter honesty of endeavour of an Alan Walker to degrees of talent which he would readily admit he lacks; you need, in effect, match-winners. A dressing-room of Alan Walkers will offer a vast reservoir of commitment and enthusiasm, but it will not perhaps have the ability to deliver the killer punch.

Twenty-five years ago, before the proliferation of one-day games and the ever-increasing emphasis on winning, having eleven players with the pride to perform in front of tiny Championship crowds on wet Thursdays at Northampton might well have been enough to sustain a club through the six days of a playing week. The need now is to combine this with the spectacular talent which can win you the game on the seventh day, be it knock-out semi-final, key Sunday League match or the vital fixture in a Championship title bid. At the same time, quite obviously, the influence of this match-winning talent cannot be so disruptive that it prevents adequate levels of achievement through the remainder of the week. Here again is the problem of balance, the theme which, perhaps before all others, underlies professional cricket.

There have, of course, been other, very different, ways of addressing the issue than seeking to keep the dressing-room together. In 1987 Ian Greig was persuaded out of retirement in Australia to accept the Surrey captaincy; the club had clearly thought hard about the kind of man they wanted, and Greig took the job very much on his own terms. His side soon came to be built around six players under the age of 25, and within two years of his arrival he had cleared from the dressing-room three highly prominent members of the First XI. Of these, the dismissal of 'Jack' Richards was one of the most remarkable in modern cricket and must have left many of the game's followers widely bemused. Richards had just passed his 30th birthday and was representing England in a Test match less than six weeks before the end of what proved to be his final season. As a fast-scoring wicket-keeper/batsman he might have helped a new county towards one-day success for five years to come, yet no club signed him. Richards was allowed to depart first-class cricket and completely disappear – to the Netherlands, in fact.

The problems at the Oval were less well known even than those at Lord's; as supporters began to digest the implications of Richards's demise, it must have occurred to some that professional cricketers were astonishingly adept at keeping their own counsel. Whatever the merits of Greig's approach, it might be thought that, before the coveted acquisition of Waqar Younis in 1990, he had left himself with a rather anonymous team. If English cricket for the established professional involves a measure of day-to-day compromise, clearly there were some defects in the dressing-room for Greig which were beyond concession, even where this entailed medium-term decline for the team.

Surrey's tribulations may well have been exceptionally severe, and the pattern of group development will not usually lead to such terminal confrontation. Careers start in a climate of restrained benignity. The professional is expected to learn quickly and think for himself; to confirm, in effect, his right to exist in the first-team dressing-room. Thereafter he becomes what he becomes. His quirks and his eccentricities are granted a qualified tolerance, whether happily tendered or with extreme reluctance for the good of the team.

And at what stage, if any, in his colleagues' eyes, will the professional have been fully made? Not, perhaps, while still described as a 'good bowler' or 'great bat' alone. Northamptonshire's Nick Cook has a curious way of combining mild lines with vehement delivery, and of certain cricketers he will passionately observe: 'He is a sound man.' 'Sound' perhaps in its classic sense — ethically correct; honest.

TWO

The Profile of an Eleven

Most discussions of the factors which have lent great cricket teams their eminence invoke at some stage the idea of balance. A side's composition may be approached in several different ways. It would, for example, be possible to break down a batting line-up into its constituent parts and define what each element is seeking to do under a given set of circumstances. Similarly, the various types of bowling can be classified and then dissected to reveal precisely what is contributed by the parts to the whole. On its own, however, neither analysis will suffice. Of far more significance is the notion of relationship, the relative weight which is to be attached to the two sides of the game, batting and bowling, and the nature of the connection which exists between them.

For a County Championship campaign, as opposed to one-day games in which the number of all-rounders or ersatz all-rounders will be vital, almost all sides will contain five batsmen, a wicket-keeper and four bowlers. The only consistent contemporary exception is Lancashire, who in 1990 were able to play three all-rounders, Wasim Akram, Mike Watkinson and Phil DeFreitas, in the middle order, and so in consequence only four specialist batsmen. Such a happy luxury enabled them to turn the complication of including a captain perhaps not fully worth his place as batsman, bowler or all-rounder into a positive advantage.

This, however, makes only ten players, and it is upon the precise role of the eleventh man that selection so frequently turns. The minimum number of men who will be required to bowl for a county in the great majority of matches in a long Championship season is not arbitrary, but is determined by the amount of work that will have to be completed on any given day, without that work so debilitating a bowler that his long-term effectiveness is impaired. In the Championship, then, the invariable need will be for five men to share the bowling.

However, if the daily workload was not 110 overs, as it presently is, but 150, one or more additional players would probably be prevailed upon to develop their ability to bowl. In Test matches where, quantitatively at least, the daily demands can be anything up to 35 per cent less severe, it has become quite commonplace to find only four-man attacks.

This does not in itself automatically solve the problem of the eleventh man, however, for some consideration will have to be given to the effect on the batting that the inclusion of a fifth bowler will have. If it is the case that the employment of five bowlers leaves the side consistently short of sufficient runs to win games, then simply meeting the physical demands of a day's play will have compromised the team's ability to compete. The classic answer to this dilemma, of course, has been an emphasis on the key role of the all-rounder, and selection is a far easier process if a captain has available to him one or more such players on the county staff. The all-rounder provides both a five-man attack and the certainty of six front-line batsmen for whom significant support may exist at Nos. 7 and 8 in the line-up depending on the batting abilities of the wicket-keeper and/or other bowlers.

The problem, however, is that in the present Championship there are at most only fourteen or fifteen genuine or potential all-rounders, and Lancashire and Northamptonshire have six between them. This includes those players who, although they have not made a great volume of runs in their careers, have shown a consistent ability to act as top-order batsmen when the circumstances have demanded it. There might be debate, for example, over the status of Watkinson and DeFreitas, or even over Malcolm Marshall who does in fact hold an all-rounder's remit in the Hampshire side. While it is true that these players do not regularly score heavily enough to suggest that they could be played as batsmen proper, it is also the case that they have not in fact been required to; they have instead tried to meet the more specific demands on No. 6 batsmen to stay for 30 or so overs after a collapse or make quick runs when needed. By the very strictest criteria, then, the count of all-rounders in English cricket might fall below ten.

If scarcity alone prevents the all-rounder from becoming the ever-present answer to problems of balance in a side, the counties are ill-advised to try to manufacture such a player simply for the sake of fulfilling the dictates of an ideal formula. Although Test cricket is not wholly comparable, in that sides will be as concerned not to lose as they are to win, England have sometimes been in danger of making the need for an all-rounder into something of a fetish. Since 1950 gaps in the sequences which saw Trevor Bailey, Tony Greig and Ian Botham hold almost assured places in the team were often filled by all-rounders adequate for the role at county level, but not so suited to Tests; Barry Knight, Richard Hutton, Chris Cowdrey and Greig's brother, Ian, come most easily to mind. A similar concern for late middle-order runs retarded the early Test careers of certain wicket-keepers, Alan Knott and 'Jack' Russell for example, whose alleged lack of batting ability led to inferior specialists such as Jim Parks and John Murray being preferred; the same pattern might also be detected in the repeated choice of spinners who can bat, such as Fred Titmus, David Allen or Vic Marks, ahead of specialists like Pat Pocock or John Childs.

All these examples imply a level of compromise in Test selection imposed by varying degrees of necessity; the caution which they indicate, whether this be termed timidity or realism, is apparent in the Championship too. A more bold response entails the second classic approach, which insists upon the primary importance of a five-man attack which can dismiss opponents twice, whether or not one of the five bowlers happens to be an all-rounder. This has been the successful Middlesex attitude of the last fifteen years and, given adequate batting, it is particularly suited to a Championship points system which now rewards victory absolutely: nothing is gained from the draw and no penalty is incurred for defeat.

Crucial here is the notion of relativity in batting strength. There can be no abstract definition, after all, of what constitutes a good total: a side which trusts its attack to dismiss opponents regularly for scores of 225 or so needs only the consistent ability to make more runs in reply, even if the ostensibly low scores involved reveal an apparent weakness in batting. The Middlesex side of the early and mid-1980s, based on only five front-line batsmen, did indeed average all-out scores of around 250, but the opposition were commonly bowled out more cheaply than this, and Middlesex thus gained sufficient victories to win the Championship. Similarly, Middlesex's Championship-winning side of 1990, a summer of record-breaking scoring, was not statistically amongst the strongest batting teams in the country. Placing great reliance on five specialist batsmen, who between them made 7,961 runs, Middlesex accepted an average contribution from its bowlers of only 20 runs each per innings, a contribution which would have been about 25 per cent lower in the less bat-dominated seasons of the 1980s.

Even more pertinent, perhaps, is the case of Warwickshire. Given the Championship points structure, a side could hypothetically lose half of its matches but still finish in the top five of the table should it win seven or eight of the remainder. In both 1988 and 1990 only one county was statistically weaker in batting than Warwickshire; in each of these seasons the team as a whole averaged less per innings with the bat than they allowed the opposition with the ball, 13 less per innings in 1988 and 28 less in 1990. More matches were lost in those two years than were won, yet Warwickshire finished sixth in 1988 and fifth in 1990. The explanation for this apparent irregularity is that the county's five-man attack was consistently amongst the most penetrative in the country; as long as, half of the time, the batsmen could ensure sufficient runs at least to compete, a high percentage of wins would follow.

If the deployment of a genuine five-man attack represents the positive option, the need for sufficient runs to support the bowling effort cannot simply be left to take care of itself. The Warwickshire example makes this clear; they did not, after all, finish top in the seasons quoted, but fifth and sixth. It is no coincidence that the most successful recent exponents of this classic strategy have each retained batsmen of the highest and most reliable stature as their overseas player, Essex with Allan Border and then Mark Waugh, Middlesex with Desmond Haynes and Worcestershire with Graeme Hick. In each case the choice was supported by the existence of considerable bowling resources in the respective clubs: given the general shortage of match-winning bowlers in England, most other counties are obliged to seek the signing of an overseas fast bowler instead. A batsman alone, however great, will not bring success to a weak bowling side, as the instance of the prolific Jimmy Cook at Somerset would confirm.

In 1990 ten of the seventeen county sides consistently based their teams around genuine, wicket-taking five-man attacks, relying on an all-rounder for the extra runs or on bowlers who could make scores when needed. Yorkshire and Middlesex, for example, looked to Phil Carrick and John Emburey for these additional runs, each side also having a wicket-keeper, Richard Blakey and Paul Downton, who batted well. The other counties put out, in effect, four-man attacks with a fifth bowler who could hold up an end without really threatening to take wickets.

This fifth bowler's role might be shared between two or more team members rather than restricted to a single, nominated player. In the three seasons 1988–90 Gloucestershire employed Phil Bainbridge and Jeremy Lloyds for some 500 overs or so between them per season, although neither were expected to gain a bowler's return of wickets. Together they had the low strike rate of one dismissal every 15 overs. As their bowling powers have declined, a similar role has been played by Ian Greig at Surrey and Chris Cowdrey at Kent, while Glamorgan's policy in 1990 was to rely upon a combination of one or more of Viv Richards, Geoff Holmes, Michael Cann and Adrian Dale. Players in this mould are, or have become, essentially batsmen who can bowl to contain and give the spearhead a chance to recuperate: they must be distinguished from specialist stock bowlers, such as Derbyshire's Alan Warner, Hampshire's Cardigan Connor or Surrey's Mark Feltham, who, although they do not expect five-wicket hauls, do bowl in anticipation of getting people out.

Because the counties rarely feel that they can afford any more than one specialist spinner under present Championship conditions, the 'manufactured' fifth member of the attack will sometimes act as a tight, containing slow bowler. The absence of circumstances in which a spinner is likely to achieve match-winning figures dictates that there will be an imbalance in the team if a second specialist is played, unless he is of the highest quality; at the same time some insurance against unforeseen circumstance, and certainly some variety, will at least be offered by the batsmen who can provide acceptable slow bowling. Viv Richards, both Peter Willey and Laurie Potter at Leicestershire and Jeremy Lloyds fall into this category while, in more of a sixth bowler's capacity, Graeme Hick and Rob Bailey are increasingly encouraged to develop their spin. Before regaining Geoff Miller from Essex, Derbyshire persisted throughout the 1988 season in an attempt to convert their opening batsman Peter Bowler into just such a tight spinner.

It would be unfair to infer from these examples that the teams cited are necessarily more defensively minded than others. It is not the case that all these counties would abide by their four-man bowling strategies, making their eleventh man an extra batsman, if they had unlimited playing resources. Test selection of this kind, as practised in 1990 by India and New Zealand, almost certainly does betray a safety-first attitude; but a county eleven can only be assembled from the talent available, which may or may not be suited to the conditions to be encountered. It would be as wrong to become fixated with the need for a specialist fifth bowler, irrespective of his quality, as it is to be obsessive about all-rounders.

Gloucestershire, for example, with a front-line quartet prior to 1991 of Courtney Walsh or Terry Alderman, David Lawrence, Kevin Curran and David Graveney, were more able than most sides to dismiss their opponents twice; what they lacked was the weight of runs to make this count. Even Essex, despite the presence of a genuine all-rounder in Derek Pringle, have on occasion entered games relying on some permutation of Graham Gooch, Mark Waugh, John Stephenson and Nadeem Shahid to support the four main bowlers in circumstances where it was anticipated that runs would be vital. Given that there are always players unavailable through injury or loss of form, the selection of the eleventh man is not usually about keeping faith with agreed principles, but about choosing between two actual players of known comparative merits. Is an out-of-form or inexperienced specialist likely to take wickets which will be beyond the non-specialist fifth bowler; will those wickets be significantly more beneficial to the side than the runs of the batsman to be omitted?

Sides sufficiently endowed with talent to relieve a captain of such pragmatic decisions are fortunate indeed. Theoretically, a side which wants to win games for itself, rather than relying on the generosity of opposing teams to offer run chases or pursue difficult last-innings targets, will place the emphasis on its attack, and will select the players who can bowl sides out. As a generalisation, Championships are won by specialisation, and the key specialists are bowlers. As soon as these tenets are applied, however, there are complications to consider. However formidable his bowlers, a captain will not relish leading a side which contains five No. 11s fighting to see who bats at No. 7.

It is doubtful, for example, whether even as admirably correct and skilled a side as the 1990–91 Australians could maintain so weak a tail as Terry Alderman, Carl Rackemann or Mike Whitney and Bruce Reid without the exceptional strength of their top order; if a batsman was injured or retired one would expect to see perhaps the all-rounder Simon O'Donnell selected ahead of a superior bowler. Teams will rarely wish to carry more than one player who cannot bat at all, and even this is far from ideal. When things become very tense in a match, a captain's freedom is disconcertingly constrained by the presence in the line-up of a recognised 'rabbit' such as Kevin Jarvis, Nottinghamshire's Andy Afford or Mark Robinson. He knows that effectively he has only three wickets left when the sixth batsman is dismissed, and this can lend an appreciably different tone to a team's thinking in a run chase or even to the thinking of middle-order batsmen when trying to increase the tempo.

For the sake of the discussion of the best balance between bat and ball in the various county staffs, it is possible to compare the actual Championship tables for 1989 and 1990 with tables which indicate the respective strengths of the counties in the two different departments. In each case the final figure in the plus or minus column shows the discrepancy between a side's actual position and its standing in the category concerned.

1989

Actual Final Table

1	Worcs
2	Essex
3	Middx
4	Lancs
5	Northants
6=	Derby
6=	Hants
8	Warwicks
9	Gloucs
10	Sussex
11	Notts
12	Surrey
13	Leics
14	Somerset
15	Kent
16	Yorks
17	Glam

Batting Average Totals

1	Sussex	316	+9
2	Kent	314	+3
3	Essex	313	−1
4	Somerset	306	+10
5	Worcs	299	−4
6	Hants	282	—
7	Surrey	281	+5
8=	Lancs	278	−4
8=	Middx	278	−5
10	Notts	276	+1
11	Warwicks	262	−3
12	Northants	261	−7
13	Yorks	256	+3
14	Leics	253	−1
15	Glam	252	+2
16	Gloucs	239	−7
17	Derby	227	−11

Bowling Average Opposition Totals

1	Worcs	214	—
2	Middx	232	+1
3	Essex	235	−1
4	Warwicks	249	+4
5	Lancs	250	−1
6	Derby	263	—
7	Hants	267	−1
8	Northants	269	−3
9	Gloucs	271	—
10	Leics	275	+3
11	Notts	278	—
12	Yorks	298	+4
13	Surrey	337	−1
14	Sussex	338	−4
15	Glam	349	+2
16	Somerset	354	−2
17	Kent	442	−2

Innings Advantage

		Batting	Bowling	+/−	
1	Worcs	299	214	+85	—
2	Essex	313	235	+78	—
3	Middx	278	232	+46	—
4	Lancs	278	250	+28	—
5	Hants	282	267	+15	+1
6	Warwicks	262	249	+13	+2
7	Notts	276	278	−2	+4
8	Northants	261	269	−8	−3
9=	Leics	253	275	−22	+4
9=	Sussex	316	338	−22	+1
11	Gloucs	239	271	−32	−2
12	Derbys	227	263	−36	−6
13	Yorks	256	298	−42	+3
14	Somerset	306	354	−48	—
15	Surrey	281	337	−56	−3
16	Glam	252	349	−97	+1
17	Kent	314	442	−128	−2

1990

Actual Final Table

1. Middx
2. Essex
3. Hants
4. Worcs
5. Warwicks
6. Lancs
7. Leics
8. Glam
9. Surrey
10. Yorks
11. Northants
12. Derby
13. Gloucs
14. Notts
15. Somerset
16. Kent
17. Sussex

Batting Average Totals

1	Somerset	490	+14
2	Essex	464	—
3	Surrey	443	+6
4	Worcs	433	—
5	Lancs	416	+1
6	Hants	415	−3
7	Middx	383	−6
8	Glam	368	—
9	Northants	366	+2
10	Kent	339	+6
11	Gloucs	332	+2
12	Yorks	321	−2
13	Derby	319	−1
14	Leics	316	−7
15	Notts	313	−4
16	Warwicks	311	−11
17	Sussex	302	—

Bowling Average Opposition Totals

1	Middx	330	—
2	Lancs	334	+4
3	Worcs	337	+1
4	Warwicks	339	+1
5	Derby	342	+7
6	Gloucs	352	+7
7	Hants	354	−4
8	Surrey	361	+1
9	Leics	364	−2
10	Northants	384	+1
11	Essex	387	−9
12	Notts	408	+2
13	Yorks	421	−3
14	Kent	425	+2
15	Somerset	431	—
16	Glam	465	−8
17	Sussex	471	—

Innings Advantage

		Batting	Bowling	+/−	
1	Worcs	433	337	+96	+3
2=	Lancs	416	334	+82	+4
2=	Surrey	443	361	+82	+7
4	Essex	464	387	+77	−2
5=	Hants	415	354	+61	−2
5=	Somerset	490	431	+61	+10
7	Middx	383	330	+53	−6
8	Northants	316	384	−18	+3
9	Gloucs	332	352	−20	+4
10	Derby	319	342	−23	+2
11	Warwicks	311	339	−28	−6
12	Leics	316	364	−48	−5
13	Kent	339	425	−86	+3
14	Notts	313	408	−95	—
15	Glam	368	465	−97	−7
16	Yorks	321	421	−100	−6
17	Sussex	302	471	−169	—

Scores based on actual Championship averages of county staffs. To take account of byes and leg-byes, some 6–7 per cent should be added to totals.

The statistics are extremely revealing, far more so than is usually the case with the game's abundant records; the fullest discussion of their significance might be a chapter in itself. The key, however, is perhaps the demonstrable connection between bowling ability and Championship success. In the tables for 1989 the correlation is especially clear: on average there is a difference of just two places between a county's relative bowling strength and its actual Championship position, a marginal discrepancy which contrasts markedly with an average difference of five places in the batting table. Similar tables for the majority of seasons in the last decade tell much the same story.

In 1990 the force of the link was diminished for the first time in many years, but it is still quite apparent. The tables for that season reflect a preponderance of pitches so 'good' that they nullified some of the advantage enjoyed by the best attacks. However, even for 1990, there are only four real anomalies in the bowling table, and each is readily explained. Derbyshire were deducted 25 points for a sub-standard pitch which distorts the picture; without that penalty their final Championship position would have been eighth, a far closer reflection of their bowling strength. Glamorgan, despite one of the weakest attacks, finished so high in the actual Championship table because they gained three of their five victories in successful run chases on the last day of a match. The mismatch between the respective positions in the two tables of Gloucestershire and Essex is much more interesting, and highlights very strongly the inconsistency which attended their seasons. Gloucestershire failed to win any of their first thirteen games and then, as the batsmen at last did the bowlers justice, won four of the remaining nine. For their part, Essex gained seven of their eight victories in a mid-season sequence of ten games. In this period Neil Foster took 49 wickets and, as in Essex sides of old, each member of an inexperienced, injury-depleted and out-of-form attack contributed crucial supporting returns at vital times. A bowling table restricted to that eight-week period alone would have found Essex at the head of the list.

The Derbyshire record in 1989 and the Leicestershire record in 1990 again show the way in which strong bowling can compensate for weak batting; conversely, the inability of strong batting alone to make a material difference to Championship success is clear in the figures for Sussex and Kent in 1989, Surrey in 1990 and Somerset in both years. At the end of the 1990 season some surprise was expressed when Warwickshire, faced with a choice between fast bowler Allan Donald and Tom Moody as their overseas player, elected to release the latter, a batsman who had made 866 runs for the side in just seven appearances. The tables perhaps explain the county's thinking.

Those who are familiar with the usual make-up of county sides, and with the pitches upon which they play, will find much food for thought in these comparative statistics. Our intention so far has been to set the idea of balance at the forefront of the discussion of team profiles. Having emphasised the whole, we may now move to the parts.

Northamptonshire's former scorer, the late Jack Mercer, one of *Wisden*'s Cricketers of the Year in 1927, used to observe with some feeling that 'really, there is only one new ball'. By this he meant that the batsmen who face the second new ball do not confront the same difficulties as those presented at the start of a match or, to a lesser degree, the start of an innings. Not only will the opposition lack the same keenness, but the game will also have assumed a pattern. Players facing the second new ball have both a context for their efforts and the knowledge gained from what has happened so far, so that they are not seeking to establish the tone of their side's performance, but are batting in the light of goals which have by now become apparent. To an extent, this is true of everyone who comes in after the first wicket has fallen. But the openers are the players who are asked to make the first exploration: only the openers initiate the pattern of play.

For this reason, players who go in first should be those best equipped, technically and mentally, to combat the peculiar demands of the unknown. However expert at reading a pitch cricketers may think themselves to be, conditions are only ever fully revealed in the opening hour or so of play. Equally, the attitude of the opposition, whether aggressive and competitive or for some reason frivolous, cannot be guessed in advance. If the pitch is to prove helpful, or the attack inspired, then this will be most evident when the ball is new and hard with a crisp seam to produce swifter and more pronounced movement.

There is in these circumstances a great dependence on

technique. The opener needs to play straight, seeking to return the ball whence it came rather than hitting through the line with drives or across it with cuts. Batsmen who tend to play away from their body, scoring runs in a wider arc (from cover point to mid-wicket) will not technically make reasonable openers. The ability to play between mid-off and mid-on, then, is essential; yet this is not a roundabout way of demanding that openers need to be defensive and temperamentally dour. Players like Larkins and, latterly in his career, the left-handed Chris Broad of Nottinghamshire are undoubtedly attacking batsmen, but both remain fine openers because the main source of their early-innings runs is precisely that area to either side of the bowler's follow-through.

Tim Curtis of Worcestershire provides an instance of an opener who lacks the best of techniques but who has always been blessed with a temperament ideal for his role. When out of form, he would not be as capable as some of getting by on the basics alone. His technical limitations were exposed by quality bowling in the 1989 Ashes series, and, typically, he responded to this severe test of his confidence by working very hard and intelligently to develop the fundamentals of a sound technique to ally to his opener's mentality. The converse of Curtis would be the player who is technically an opening bat but who will be too ambitious too soon in his innings. The opener requires a definite solidity of thought; because of this, it is probably true that most players would probably seek to bat at No. 3, 4 or 5 rather than open. Openers become openers either because a captain has identified their talents and outlook as appropriate or because other candidates are lacking and different players are prevailed upon to accept the job.

As there are two elements, the one technical and the other psychological, to the make-up of an opener, so there are different phases to his task. After perhaps 20 or so overs, when the new-ball bowlers have completed their spells and the attack has adopted different perspectives, the openers begin to reassess their situation. The scoreboard can now be viewed more positively in terms of appropriate targets to be met by certain stages of the innings. It is always easier for a middle-order batsman to come in with 120 runs on the board than it is at 15–2. At the former score he arrives with the psychological advantage already gained and the stage cleared for his abilities; he has been able to note both the conditions and the full breadth of the opposing attack. By assisting him in this process, the openers fulfil a further vital function. When a wicket falls or during an interval they can inform their team-mates what awaits them and what goals may be aimed for, and in this sense the laying of a foundation entails making the structure of an innings not only easier to build, but more apparent to those who will build it.

The full role of the opener, however, goes further than this. If a player bats first in his side and averages between 35 and 40 over a season then he will often be thought to have done his job. This does not mean that it is his job to bat through the opening 100 minutes, score those 35 runs and then rest, satisfied that the innings has been securely established. Part of that mental complement to the technical prerequisites outlined above is the capacity to capitalise upon the good start. It is a generalisation, but it is reasonable to expect that, if an opener has successfully countered the new ball and denied the opposition the early initiative, he will then at least try to bat through most of the day. In a Championship innings which is to realise perhaps 360 in 100 overs, the opener can be more than satisfied with a not out score of 140, while a No. 5 batsman's role in the same context might more typically be to achieve a faster, more flowing 70 or 80. The responsibility, in short, is to complete the job which has been started.

The more runs he can find and, with gradual acceleration, the longer he can stay at the crease, the easier the opener should make it for a newcomer to arrive in favourable circumstances, with the opposition disenchanted and defensively minded. When Alan Fordham made his maiden first-class century for Northamptonshire at the Oval in 1988 he was joined, at 91–2, by David Capel. On a dull pitch, Fordham became concerned in mid-afternoon that perhaps he was advancing too slowly. Capel, outscoring his partner by more than two to one in a stand that was to add 119, constantly reassured the inexperienced opener that he was doing precisely the right thing, while himself making a typically selfless middle-order 81 at the other end. The wisdom of Fordham remaining at the crease in conditions which, if not difficult, were consistently testing was shown when Capel fell and the next two batsmen were out immediately for 7 runs between them. At the close, in a total of 298–5, Fordham was 125 not out and only the loss of two hours to rain on the second morning denied Northamptonshire the edge which his efforts would otherwise have achieved in the conditions.

We have spoken so far of the individual. But openers come out in pairs, not alone. In essence the ideal opening partnership seeks to disrupt the opposition's rhythm, both the actual lines and lengths that the bowlers wish to maintain and the settled tactics that their captain would like to pursue. A left-hand/right-hand alliance is perhaps the combination most often thought to promote this, but other blends can be equally telling: batsmen who score runs in different areas of the field (for example, a short man who eschews the hook complementing a tall man who plays well off his body), batsmen who are particularly expert in their running so that the less attacking partner can push singles and give his aggressive colleague the strike, or a back-foot player and a front-foot player. Given the modern tendency towards short-pitched new-ball bowling, the contemporary opener who is not adept at back-foot play will be exposed and his life span in the role will be brief, but two players who attack off different feet present problems to a bowler trying to establish a consistent length.

Belligerence in an opening batsman might be thought to bring sighs of dismay from men waiting to come in, and David Steele used to declare, only half in jest, that the worst period of his career was when batting No. 3 to a Northamptonshire opening pair of Alan Tait and Geoff Cook. Both were guilty of rash, youthful moments, and this, Steele alleged, turned him to cigarettes and his hair to premature whiteness. The key, however, is not to seek to impose one single, inflexible approach on the openers, but to allow their deeds to speak for themselves.

As long as openers such as Colin Milburn, Wayne Larkins, Keith Stackpole or Graham Gooch demonstrate by regular success that their talent is equal to the methods they employ, team-mates will happily concede the wisdom of their outlook. However, if attack is a matter of impetuosity alone, without an opener's awareness of his own limitations and his side's need for a firm foundation, it will not be acceptable. Larkins in particular used to relish that half an hour of batting at the end of a day which most openers resent intensely because, with plentiful gaps in the field and the bowlers committed to all-out attack, he could expect to be 40 not out at the close. His partners, in contrast, would more typically steel themselves to defend grimly against four slips and a gully, but if Larkins's bravura was perplexing for his fellow opener, it was undoubtedly more so for the opposition.

When spectators look at opening partnerships they often sense an understanding and kinship which extends well beyond life at the crease. Openers, more than any other pairing in the side – with the exception, perhaps, of spinners – convey that certain feeling of comradeship and mutual respect and, although appearances can be deceptive in cricket, there is much truth in this impression. The strength of the ties which are forged derives in the main from the common problems which the two batsmen face; empathy grows from shared adversity. Various players have various ways of forming this relationship – some through constant communication, others through a quieter trust in their partner's ability. A batsman who feels tentative under certain circumstances at the crease can grow in confidence from the self-belief his colleague imparts.

On England's 1990–91 tour of Australia, Larkins and Mike Atherton seemed to suffer from the absence of the leadership qualities and, indeed, of the pure physical presence of Graham Gooch at the other end. They are both gifted cricketers of significant experience, but they both batted with less self-assurance when paired together. This is not to say that a relationship would not have blossomed in time; but batsmen encountering common unknown problems at the start of an innings do take time to gain an awareness of how the other will cope, and it is an awareness that becomes more perceptive and enabling as it is allowed to develop. Established opening partnerships offer more to a team than the sum of two individual talents, and each member of the partnership is reluctant to see it severed before it can complete its growth. By virtue of the openers' vulnerability, there is always a chance that the partnership will stimulate not mutual support, but antipathy and irritation; certain opening alliances have markedly lacked the best qualities described above. These, however, are the exceptions: it is very rare for an established partnership to break up other than for the needs of a team.

The No. 3 batsman can never know in advance which of two main roles he will be required to play that day. He does not know whether, if the first wicket falls immediately, he will have to act as a surrogate opener or whether, coming in at 130–1, he will be part of the attacking middle order soon after reaching the crease. Ideally, therefore, he will be a fairly phlegmatic cricketer, able to cope not only with the uncertainty of his role, but with the different approaches of the two opening batsmen with whom he will share second-wicket stands for long periods of the season.

The No. 3 slot, then, is the position which perhaps calls for the greatest adaptability. It requires an ability, after the batsman has played himself in, to apply distinctly different frames of mind: he will either display a determination to supply the solid base which the opener has been unable to build, or he will be mindful not to lose the momentum which the first wicket has created. At the technical level, this means that he must possess both a reasonable aptitude for the particular difficulties of the opener's role, and sufficient freedom of shot to expand upon the good start.

These two possibilities are alive each time a new innings begins; for batsmen at Nos. 4, 5 and 6, the variety of different demands is appreciably less marked. There is a considerable distinction between 70–1 and, say, 150–3. At 70–1, the loss of a second wicket could change the balance of a game and threaten that, should a third wicket go down, much of the early good work will have been squandered. At the same time, 70–1 is clearly an acceptable start, and it is incumbent upon the No. 3 batsman to move the innings forward. The balancing of objectives here – to ensure by consolidation that the good start is not wasted, but also to extend with judicious aggression the psychological advantage gained – is more delicate than at 150–3, by which time, barring abject collapse, a score reasonable enough to keep the side in the match should follow.

It may be wondered why, if a No. 3 is so often required to play like an opener, he does not seek to become one. Cricketers find it very difficult to come off after fielding, put on their pads and return to the middle immediately; the relaxation of only a few overs can make a significant difference. Despite the success of David Steele for England when pressed into service as an opener in 1976, he so disliked his new role that he believed any move from No. 3 would always be unhappy. Equally, the best players for the position would neither carry a secret desire to bat at No. 4 or 5 nor be reluctant conscripts from the middle order.

Graeme Hick, for example, would expressly classify himself as a No. 3, not a middle-order bat. He is desperately keen to get to the crease and take command of proceedings, but wants only the immediate respite of avoiding the need to follow the opposition out. Once Worcestershire lose a wicket, Hick takes the field probably faster than any other batsman in the Championship but, rightly, he wishes to do so on his own terms. He will have composed himself for the task ahead in the way he knows best suited to his temperament. Hick and Australia's Greg Chappell, both technically correct and straight batsmen able to dominate opposing bowlers after blunting their initial attack, provide almost perfect examples of the distinct qualities required.

Batsmen such as David Gower and Rob Bailey who have for long periods batted at No. 3 – and, indeed, scored volumes of runs there – do not seem quite so technically suited to the role. Gower's stroke-play would arguably produce the greatest dividends against a ball which is no longer moving, while Bailey's susceptibility to deliveries outside the off stump is more likely to be probed by the fields more typically set at the fall of the first wicket than those at the fall of the third. Both are to a degree 'mood' batsmen whose momentary lapses of concentration can undo them when the opposition is at its freshest and keenest; yet both are able to demoralise attacks with, in Gower's case, deft stroke-play and, in Bailey's, astonishing strength and timing of shot. This would imply that their greatest value might be in the middle order.

Much is made of the importance of the No. 3 batsman because he most obviously combines two such different approaches but, in fact, no single batting position is more crucial than any other. With regard to winning matches, insofar as batsmen can ever be said to win matches, each of the top five or six places in the order has, at varying times, a central significance. Whilst failure in the first three positions makes it difficult for a team to get the best out of its stroke-players, regular failure at Nos. 4, 5 and even 6 will prevent teams achieving actual and psychological dominance.

Consistency is of benefit in every position in the line-up, but it is arguably more important to a side's ability to stay on level terms throughout a campaign when it is displayed in the upper order. Moreover, given the part they are expected to play, it is less legitimate to ask of middle-order batsmen that they should aspire to a uniform solidity. There is a considerable difference between batting as an opener and batting at No. 4 or 5, a difference which is probably more pronounced than is generally recognised. Establishing yourself at the crease at the top of the innings is a great deal more difficult than it is lower down; the threat to the batsman's wicket is usually far more palpable and pressing, the intensity of his combat with a bowler more relentless. Nevertheless, middle-order batsmen pay for the comparative ease of their existence in other ways.

Since survival is less hazardous, the expectation is that the middle order will commit themselves to something altogether more ambitious. Indeed, at Championship level, the prime characteristic of a good middle-order batsman is an admirably unselfish pursuit of runs at a rate commensurate with the needs of the moment. This brings its own peculiar pressure. The middle-order bat must never allow the momentum to slacken, a responsibility which itself threatens his downfall if he is prepared to accept it as fully as his role dictates. This will be at a time when the gaps in the field are far fewer, and finding the boundary is consequently more difficult. For this reason it is a gross error to consider the role as in any sense a more comfortable berth.

While the top three batsmen may sometimes inwardly resent the glory which is attached to middle-order assaults on tired or second-string attacks, there is often something decidedly thankless to the task in three-day cricket on batsmen's pitches. In pursuit of batting points, runs for a declaration or runs to achieve a last-afternoon target, the middle-order player may be asked to risk sacrificing his wicket for the needs of the side three or four times more often than his top-order counterpart.

Ironically, a good start to a Championship innings can bring its own dangers to Nos. 4 and 5. As they will probably be the side's finest stroke-players, those whose ambitions may be thwarted by a hard, seaming ball but who are best able to punish a flagging and slightly dispirited attack, the success of earlier batsmen can invite a certain complacency; the inclination may be to seek dominance too soon. When Nos. 1, 2 and 3 have played well, several boundaries will have been scored, and this may give the appearance that conditions are a little better than they actually are. Similarly, the attitude and approach of the opposition can be misinterpreted, and stroke-players sometimes need to be reminded that they must still establish themselves for those few crucial opening overs before seizing the chance to display their shots. Fielding sides are given a dangerous psychological lift by the ten minutes which translate 150–3 into 160–5, and middle-order stutters of this sort are often due to Nos. 4 and 5 trying to inflict further punishment on the opponent too quickly. Such a minor collapse will not necessarily lead to a side being dismissed cheaply, since most teams today should be able to recover from 160–5 to at least 250 all out. It does, however, mean that those batsmen capable of ensuring that the big total is reached swiftly enough to set up a chance of victory are lost at exactly the wrong time.

The order in which the specialist batsmen come to the crease will sometimes be complicated by the presence in the side of a genuine all-rounder. Where the all-rounder does not bat at No. 6, the need to accommodate him higher in the order can mean that a specialist will find himself batting at No. 6, where he becomes an extension of the authentic middle order. The introduction of four-day cricket over the last four seasons has enabled batsmen at No. 6, or even 7, to reveal abilities which few recognised them to have. This in itself indicates how difficult it is for a specialist to bat so late in the order in a three-day game. Opportunities to build an innings here are so limited, and the requirement for unselfishness so pronounced, that a particularly keen sense of team-spiritedness is demanded. It is a position often associated with veterans who have nothing further to prove in the game, whose experience makes them especially astute at judging whether the situation requires 30 rapid runs or stubborn defence to prolong the innings.

Jim Yardley, in seven seasons at Northampton after joining the county from Worcester as his 30th birthday beckoned, was of so unorthodox and severely limited a style that it was difficult to justify his batting higher than No. 6. In that position, however, he scored vital quick runs for his side at important junctures by virtue of both this very unorthodoxy, which made it difficult to set containing fields for him, and his wholehearted team approach. Brian Hardie, towards the end of his eighteen summers with Essex, sometimes played in a similar role down the order. For young cricketers coming into the game, however, and even for players such as Jeremy Lloyds and Laurie Potter who have never really gained a consistent chance to bat in the middle order proper, three-day cricket offers very few opportunities to demonstrate batting ability to the full. Quite naturally, it is easier for players to accept, and indeed relish, this role if their main contribution is felt to be in other departments. For the specialist batsman, the lot of the No. 6 is such that he can hardly win: if the top order has scored runs, he is expected to take risks; if it has failed, conditions are probably poor and survival will be difficult.

Ideally, the lower middle order – Nos. 6, 7 and even 8 – will play an essential part in adding the late flourish which can take a side to an acceptable all-out total or to a declaration sooner rather than later. In terms of winning matches, however, the late middle-order batsmen are frequently more significant than is widely realised. Not only can they take a team to success on the final afternoon, but on difficult pitches they may provide sufficient extra runs to ensure a first-innings lead sizeable enough to set up the bid for victory. The Essex team of the late 1970s and early 1980s contained lower middle-order bats who were not recognised as full all-rounders – men like Stuart Turner, the wicket-keepers Neil Smith and, after him, David East and even, at No. 8 or 9, slow left-armer Ray East. All these players were quite capable of putting together crucial 25s and 30s.

On poor pitches, given the strength of an Essex attack which could be expected to dismiss top-order batsmen relatively cheaply, such runs would prove just as valuable as the

50s and 60s of men higher up, if not more so. The same is similarly true of the contemporary Essex side, Mike Garnham and Neil Foster often finding runs when they are most needed, and of Worcestershire, who can usually rely on opportune contributions from Steve Rhodes, Richard Illingworth, Phil Newport and, indeed, Graham Dilley should the top order fail. Middlesex, although they have been ably served in this regard by John Emburey, Phil Edmonds and Paul Downton, have more usually relied far more centrally on their batsmen. Middlesex batsmen are asked to score, if not a lot of runs, then sufficient for the county's needs given the balanced excellence of the specialist attack.

The key attribute of the late middle order and tail is not batting competence *per se*, but an awareness of the circumstances in which one must play to the utmost of one's ability. A player like Ray East was no more naturally gifted than many other No. 9s in the Championship, but the philosophy of the Essex team, its collective grasp of a game, consistently led him to maximise his talent at precisely the times when it was most necessary. Such a grasp goes beyond questions of mere proficiency in a side's batting balance to the pivotal issues of attitude and understanding.

It is important, then, not so much to quantify the percentage of a total which the two halves of an innings should produce, as to emphasise that the bottom order must make critical runs when required. This is not as obvious as it sounds. Clearly, if a side finds itself at 90–5, every possible further addition should be fought for. Similarly, when a side reaches 300–6 after 85 overs it should be apparent that, if it is only to bat on for another forty minutes or so, as many runs as possible should come in that time even if the team is bowled out in the process. Perhaps more difficult to apprehend is the centrality of those runs which take a team from, say, 160–6 to 240 all out in a match where this will prove the highest score and, as such, probably a winning one.

An analysis of the fall of wickets through two complete Championship seasons in the mid-1980s reveals the following average breakdown of runs per partnership. These averages are lower than would be expected on the batting pitches stipulated for the early 1990s, building to a team total of 288 as opposed to the imbalanced 372 of 1990. However, the proportion of the overall score realised by each wicket remains relevant.

1st wkt – 39 (score 39–1);	6th – 27 (208–6);
2nd – 33 (72–2);	7th – 30 (238–7);
3rd – 37 (109–3);	8th – 20 (258–8);
4th – 36 (145–4);	9th – 17 (275–9);
5th – 36 (181–5);	10th – 13 (288 all out).

There are two surprising elements here. Between them, the sixth and seventh wickets contribute about 80 per cent of the runs achieved by any other two consecutive partnerships higher in the order; and the ratio between top-order and bottom-order runs is 63:37, a closer balance than many cricketers would probably suspect.

Both findings reflect the trend over the last twenty years towards increased runs in the late order, a trend which owes much to the points structure in the Championship, less in terms of batting bonus points than of the fact that all spoils go to the victor. Run chases have consequently become more frequent, and sides commonly pursue targets to the fall of the eighth or ninth wicket. Even more significant than this, however, is the prevalence of one-day cricket, which now regularly obliges the tail to contrive runs under pressure.

It is also the case that pitches today are much more bland and flat towards the end of an innings. As batsmen in the tail have found survival both easier and more necessary, so techniques have improved and confidence has grown. Moreover, the trend tends to confirm itself: as certain sides have developed run-scoring depth, so others have sought to emulate them by requiring their lower orders to practise. The attitude, in short, has become that the majority of professional cricketers should at least know one end of a bat from the other.

Yet the ability of tails to wag on bland Championship pitches is often of dubious benefit to the three-day game. It is now quite common for Nos. 8 to 11 to frustrate their opponents as they edge their team total towards 300, but unfortunately they will often do so too slowly for the interests of a 'natural' conclusion to the fixture. Tactics here are sometimes more misguided than the traditional tail-ender's readiness to throw the bat. When conditions are so favourable to batting that it proves relatively easy for the tail to survive, the game would almost always be better served if the score were advanced at a faster rate.

If a side contains an all-rounder he will almost certainly bat at No. 4, 5 or 6, more usually in one of the latter two positions. The role involves such physical and mental strain that it would be entirely unreasonable to expect a player both to perform in the top three and to bowl 70 overs a week with any degree of efficiency. Nobody currently fulfils such a role in the Championship, nor have they done for years. The nearest equivalent might be the use of a wicket-keeper as a top-order batsman, as Yorkshire have employed Richard Blakey and as, in recent seasons, Middlesex have experimented with Paul Downton and Derbyshire with Bernie Maher. Even here, the conjunction of highly specialist roles is unusual enough to prompt frequent comment. In Test cricket abroad where, for the home player, individual matches can be the culmination of two or three weeks unhindered preparation, the combination is more feasible but still remains rare.

Why are there so few all-rounders left in the game? The answer may seem to follow quite directly from the points made above: the demands of an all-rounder's workload alone are prohibitive. More than this, however, paucity can perpetuate itself: unless a player is very talented in both roles and determined to develop each one, he may well be advised early in his career to take the easier option. In this sense the key is perhaps the player's own self-assessment; a cricketer such as South African Eddie Barlow was passionately drawn to the idea of opening both batting and bowling and would have felt profoundly deprived had either challenge been denied him. All-rounders such as Barlow, Ian Botham, Mike Procter and Imran Khan seem born to their role; their greatness derives from the fact that they were indeed all-rounders, at all times part of the game, and they would not have achieved such eminence had they devoted themselves to becoming better specialists.

The case of Northamptonshire's David Capel illustrates the kind of thinking which many players of lesser all-round ability must entertain. In his heart Capel has not been an all-rounder for some time; he openly declares a deep love for batting but has long regarded bowling as necessary hard labour for the good of the cause. He fears that it places too great a stress on a frail body, and that a career is shortened by all-round responsibilities. Equally important, his own Test ambitions have been retarded by the public perception of him as an all-rounder; this has perhaps detracted from a wider awareness of his formidable middle-order batting skills.

If this is the feeling of as gifted a player as Capel, it is hardly surprising that cricketers of lesser talent make an early decision to concentrate on one skill alone. Most professionals will at some stage have both batted and bowled but, realising that one of these skills will not be maintained without debilitating effort, they opt for the realisation of their fullest potential in a single sphere. If they choose to discard their bowling, their ability in that department will decline alarmingly, since success with the ball can require three or four seasons of constant first-class practice. There are only eleven places to be filled, whether in a county team or for one's country; unless he feels entirely at home in an all-round role, the professional's natural inclination will be to establish the likeliest path to a place and devote himself to following it.

In a five-man attack, the classic balance would once have comprised two new-ball bowlers, a back-up medium-pacer of tight control and two spinners. Today it is far from certain that there will be even one spinner on show; if one is played, he is most likely to be a slow left-armer. The conventional wisdom which asserted that 'if three seamers cannot do the job, four never will' is, in present conditions, untrue; modern theory has it that seam quartets will usually do better than attacks which retain balance merely for the sake of it. It is still the case that a side will be exposed if it contains pace alone, but one spinner is usually thought to offer variation enough. In 1990 only three counties consistently played two genuine spinners, one breaking from off, the other from leg, to operate in tandem.

Most spinners are not only less likely to take wickets, they are less likely even to bowl for wickets than their faster colleagues. Whereas, especially in the first innings, the front-line three or four seamers are virtually guaranteed their 20 to 25 overs, the spinner will not necessarily get on for any length of time at all. Pitches are so against him that a seamer, even a 'phantom' of military medium pace, offers his captain a better chance of taking a wicket. This has led to the development of the spinner who can either provide something more for the side than his bowling alone or who can bowl with expert containment against batsmen trying to force the pace. There is, of course, something of the vicious circle about this: a spinner will not become an expert container without practice, but he cannot get practice if he is not worth his place. Peter Such's career presents a modern tale as generic as it is sad. An old-fashioned spinner of real specialist ability, he neither bats nor fields with distinction. He has moved from Nottinghamshire to Leicestershire to Essex in vain search of the opportunities which, fifteen years ago on uncovered and livelier surfaces, his gifts would certainly have brought him.

The key match-winning element in an attack, and even in a team, will be the spearhead. These days this may involve two penetrating, new-ball bowlers or one fairly venomous new-ball bowler complemented by a player of steady, nagging accuracy at the other end. Both approaches have been employed by Lancashire, who in the recent past have combined Wasim Akram or Patrick Patterson with Paul Allott's control; in 1989 the overseas strike bowler was joined by DeFreitas, when available, and Allott was kept in reserve as first change.

The extent to which the new-ball attack seeks penetration may itself dictate the depth of the stock-bowling back-up required. As the spearhead pursues wickets, so it risks a degree of punishment. The back-up bowlers, however, will wish to keep things more tight, seeking to check a rate of scoring which may have resulted from over- or underpitching in search of the attacking length. Alternatively, they may attempt to restrain the batsmen during precisely that period of respite from the more dangerous bowlers when they might otherwise try to make up lost ground. It is often at this point that the best support bowlers can themselves gain wickets. As batsmen relax a little and look for runs, so they become vulnerable to extreme accuracy or intelligent variations of line and length at brisk medium pace.

Middlesex's Norman Cowans offers a fine example of a player who, at the age of 30, has moved from spearhead to support bowling but continues to gain regular successes.

Ideally, one of these back-up men will be of a temperament prepared to accept occasional circumstances of some adversity. He may undertake a considerable workload if it is imperative to keep the spearhead fresh on an unhelpful pitch, or he may bowl with the elements against him. Max Walker's qualities in this regard made him an integral part of an Australian attack dominated by Lillee and Thomson in the 1970s; the mean reliability of Derek Pringle at Essex is exactly the foil required for Neil Foster's variety and experimentation. On good batting wickets, however, one of the arts of captaincy is to ensure that the burden is reasonably well spread between the bowlers, although some might argue that it is the contemporary lot of the restrictive spinner to bowl more than his share, in probably longer spells, when the batsmen are clearly on top. And in conditions where one particular type of bowler is appreciably assisted, he will obviously complete a greater proportion of the work.

The captain will also keep in mind that his strike bowler will need a degree of accepted special handling; for Northamptonshire to bowl Curtly Ambrose unrelentingly on a flat, unhelpful pitch at Northampton when he may prove to win the next game on a fast, bouncy strip at the Oval will be against the acknowledged interests of the side. A captain must avoid mollycoddling a bowler to the unfair detriment of the rest of the attack, while retaining a certain amount of foresight. In this sense, the distribution of 100 overs across five bowlers might permit relative shares of, say, 17 to 23 but not of 10 to 30.

Needless to say, these policies must remain flexible, not prescriptive. The essence of good captaincy is to combine an assessment of the likelihood that wickets will fall with the ability to pace the bowlers for the probable duration of an innings. To put all the eggs in the pre-lunch basket, for example, by asking new-ball bowlers to attempt spells of ten or eleven overs each, will usually make for great problems later in the day. Only success will justify the gamble, and success here probably means at least five and perhaps six wickets in the first session. For a bowler to be kept on for so long that he will be unable to return for a second spell in the afternoon, or will return as no real threat, the benefit of the tactic must be considerable.

The greatly respected Peter Van der Merwe, who led South Africa's last tour of England in 1965, claimed that a captain should always set a plan until lunch, knowing exactly when he will take bowlers off. The thinking behind this is that even if a man is taking wickets he can always be brought back for a second spell later in the session because he has been kept fresh. If pushed to the limit, however, without achieving match-winning figures, he is not likely to be successful at the second attempt. All maxims such as this in cricket can, of course, be disregarded, and on occasions a captain will be best advised to have the courage to forsake golden rules. Yet his judgement here is critical. At its best, the art of deploying an attack involves recognising the exact moment to withdraw a bowler – usually defined as after the over which precedes the one over too many. Such perfect timing is easy in retrospect; but the best captaincy anticipates the key moment and risks the criticism of those who, unable to be contradicted by subsequent events, will argue that the decision was premature.

Such a decision will often hinge on knowledge of the individual bowler. At Northampton, the side had become used to the rhythmical, smooth and energy-conserving run-up of Winston Davis over the two summers prior to the arrival of Curtly Ambrose in 1989, an approach which made him happy to bowl long, 11-over spells, especially when he was taking wickets. Ambrose, however, is temperamentally unsuited to this kind of workload and, in long spells, was relatively ineffective by a seventh or even a sixth over. Consequently, in his second season, he was rarely asked to bowl more than five overs at a time, even if his brief burst had gained two or three successes. Such sensitivity at last made Ambrose the formidable Championship opponent it had always been hoped he would become.

Yet Ambrose's aggregate workload over the season remained comparable to Davis's. In 1990 he delivered 484 overs in fourteen matches, whereas in 1988 Davis had bowled 538 in fifteen matches. Ambrose's overs, however, came in perhaps twenty or so more spells than would be normal in a summer for Davis or, indeed, most strike bowlers. To accommodate this, other bowlers were asked to operate for slightly longer or shorter periods at various times than ideally they would have liked. This, though, is the essence of teamwork in an attack conceived as a single unit: bowlers should be capable of recognising how the best interests of their side are served, just as top-order batsmen must acknowledge the merit of 40 quick runs from a No. 6. It is a matter of the attack being governed by a strategy which can win matches rather than by an inappropriate desire to ensure formal equity for all: the best professional attacks will not need powers of persuasion to make them accept a plan, but the force of the plan's logic alone.

As we have noted, one strategy which has become widespread involves a preference for the slow left-armer ahead of the off-spinner, and certainly ahead of the off-spinner who cannot bat. In 1990 there were twenty-nine slow bowlers who delivered more than 250 Championship overs. Of these, three were leg-spinners, and, although numerically the split between the remainder was exactly even, the division of labour was far more marked: slow left-armers bowled 58 per cent of deliveries, off-spinners 42 per cent. The figures reflect a broad consensus that, unless the off-spinner is an extremely good bowler (which, with one or two exceptions, means that he learnt his craft before pitches were covered), he will be far too vulnerable on both sides of the pitch. The likelihood of his getting anybody out on slow surfaces of low bounce, where close fielders are necessarily limited in number, is sadly small.

For the slow left-armer, it will remain possible to set a field that can adequately contain as well as accept the close catch. The good slow left-armer is still very highly valued in the Championship because he will be able to bowl long spells on batsmen's pitches without conceding great numbers of runs and because, should there be any turn, he is more likely to exploit it. The slow left-armer is thus operating in two complementary ways at the same time: although pitches are invariably too slow to enable him to 'run through' a side, he can maintain an off-stump line to restrict the batsmen and, especially where he gains assistance, he can make periodic breakthroughs should they seek to force the pace.

This new role of attritional slow left-armer, then, is a distinct Championship category now, often acting as the fifth member of a five-man attack. He is able to take wickets at regular, if lengthy, intervals all the way through a long spell, seeking such wickets by tying batsmen down; even if he fails to strike, he has at least arrested the opposition's momentum. The theory that spinners hunt best in pairs is still valid; the point is that the spinner rarely 'hunts' at all today in the sense traditionally intended.

Although it is a debate which has recurred throughout the game's history, the argument over the need or otherwise for a wicket-keeper to score runs has perhaps been most prominent in the last fifteen years. This has largely mirrored the disappearance of conditions which encourage attacking spin; ostensibly the requirement for specialist wicket-keeping skills is now less pronounced. Such thinking is reasonably valid, but it obscures the individuality of the part which a quality wicket-keeper plays. He is, after all, the one man in a side who can singlehandedly make the inadequate in a bowler look average and the average seem good, both by ensuring that half-chances are accepted and by masking any waywardness of length or line. The wicket-keeper who can stand up to the medium-pacer or has the knack of taking all returns on the volley compensates for real deficiencies in a team. In terms of the morale of a side and the persona it projects, these attributes are more significant than is usually acknowledged. Sub-standard wicket-keeping makes a side look poor, eroding self-respect and self-belief. Although this is perhaps also true of shoddy fielding, in general no other member of the eleven carries so concentrated a responsibility for ensuring that his team gives the impression of an efficient, professional unit.

While this assessment has recently regained ground, the amount of one-day cricket now played obliges the wicket-keeper to take his batting seriously. There was not the same incentive in the past for regular tail-end wicket-keepers such as D. A. Pullan, Laurie Johnson or Ken Goodwin to apply themselves doubly hard to batting practice. Despite Surrey's use of David Ward and Alec Stewart in 1990 as batsmen who could keep wicket, the present trend is moving back to the belief that the greatest value is in a genuine wicket-keeper who can bat reasonably on occasion. At Derby, Bernie Maher has given way to Karl Krikken, Warwickshire's Geoff Humpage was superseded by Piran Holloway and Keith Piper, and at Sussex Ian Gould became a No. 6 batsman in deference to the specialist skills of Peter Moores. However, it is inconceivable today that wicket-keepers will be allowed to neglect their batting with the excuse that it diverts attention from their principal interest.

Wicket-keepers also now assume, as a conscious part of their game, that they will be the focus of their team's attempts to keep spirits high and encourage the efforts of the bowler. Cricket, overall, has become a lot more vocal, and in this the wicket-keeper acts as choir master. His despondency probably has a greater power to communicate itself to a side than the mood of any other individual player. Increasingly, then, the wicket-keeper exercises an unseen, psychological influence and, indeed, he will blame himself if the side begins to wander.

When prepared to accept the authority to offer assessments, the confident wicket-keeper can contribute more than pure skill to his county. He is, after all, uniquely well-placed, and the need to read the pitch and detect problems in the attack is intrinsic to his game. This should make him an important contributor to team discussion both during play and in the dressing-room. Ideally, he will feel able to comment technically not only on bowling and fielding, but, in practice sessions, on the difficulties being experienced by a particular batsman.

This emphasis on the psychological and interpretative aspects of the wicket-keeper's game has assumed a distinctively modern relevance, but the question of attitude which it raises is applicable to all the roles within the team. The profile of an eleven is not only about assembling an appropriate compound of talent; were cricket as simple as that it would neither be so absorbing to watch nor, perhaps, so frequently disturbing to play.

THREE

The Sociology of Success

In the opening chapter we established the central aim of dressing-room preparation: the creation of a working harmony which can enable a group of cricketers to walk out on to a field and do justice to itself both individually and collectively. But there is a context to such efforts, a context which, despite its undoubted significance, has been strangely unexplored. The public face of a county cricket club, the eleven which plays in its name, is almost all a supporter knows. Only occasionally are there intimations of a wider world: a contest over the disposal of power erupts in Extraordinary General Meetings at Harrogate or Shepton Mallett; a batsman's character is found so fascinatingly complex that its roots are pursued in the South Yorkshire coalfield of his boyhood. A team carries more into the game than the approaches and abilities we examined earlier; there is a political and cultural dimension to cricket.

For at least ten years in British industry, commerce and public service a debate has continued over the organisation of lines of authority. The inquiry, now enthusiastically endorsed as a subject for study in courses on management science, is into those working structures and practices which might best promote efficiency and contain conflicts of interest. This is not a debate which has disturbed county cricket; there the organisation of influence remains customary, hazy and some-times quarrelsome. In the winter of 1990–91 Yorkshire set a precedent of potentially great significance by commissioning a confidential, outside consultants' report into the club. Histori-cally, however, successful forms of administration have evolved from the presence of forceful but generally benign individuals, while the working relationships which have contributed to a team's performance have emerged by a combination of foresight and chance.

The Narrow Line

In theory, it is easy to set down the approximate fabric of a county club's hierarchy, but the formulation is complicated by the fact that what appears to be a pyramid could not in practice operate as a chain of command. It can be represented in the following form:

Membership – General Committee – Secretary (or Chief Executive)
– Captain – Vice-Captain/Coach/Cricket Manager(?) – Team

Further gradations might indicate different categories of membership, perhaps, or ascribe varying degrees of prominence to separate sub-sections of players on the contracted staff. As a bald outline of potential power, however, this is probably adequate and it appears simple enough. The membership, through their theoretical ability to pass any resolution deemed appropriate at an Annual General Meeting, can determine the development of the club and, through their capacity to vote on candidates for the committee, they can also signal their approval or disapproval of any given policy. Although the ultimate sanction does reside with the members, it is clearly not the case in any short-term sense that they exercise authority; it is inconceivable, to provide an absurd illustration, that the membership could claim the right to select the team by periodic secret ballot.

Unfortunately, the above scheme conceals the actual problems of the daily exercise of power which a club has to resolve if it is to achieve the most reassuring and secure background for its team to play against. The common goal, after all, should be success on the field. So long as players feel that they are part of a club structure which genuinely and collectively pursues this and provides sincere support for their endeavours, they are more likely to play to their potential. The apparent demarcation of authority, however, is deceptive, particularly, for example, over the status of the cricket manager, a post in existence at almost half the county clubs. Other grey areas relate to the secretary or chief executive, a paid official of the club who might arguably be removed from the above representation altogether and placed in a purely administrative category; also to the general committee, an amorphous body which may comprise just one or two assertive individuals supported by a pliant majority.

As the person who, day after day, has the responsibility to lead the side itself, it is the captain who should ideally occupy the focal role in a county's structure. It cannot be stressed enough that the captain should be at the heart of all the club's cricketing decisions, in terms not only of selection and tactics, but also of those long-term policies which will dictate the future playing direction of the county's teams. The administrative machinery of a county club, often working unseen, undertakes much fruitful labour and may generate a wealth of good advice, but if it can produce the correct choice of captain, the committee will have performed its single most valuable service. From this it follows unavoidably that if, after every opportunity has been afforded and all assistance extended, the captain still proves inadequate to his task, another man will be put in his place. Decisions on whom to appoint and when, or if, to make a change are the most important a committee will ever take.

There are certain obvious reasons why captains can fail to assume the prominence which their positions demand. Some do not follow fully enough the fortunes of the Second XI and, in consequence, find themselves relying too heavily on the opinions of others. If it is through the captain that the middle-term agenda of the club should be set – its cricket strategy for the next three or four seasons, say – it is important for him to know at first hand precisely how the youngsters on the staff relate to his own thinking.

Similarly, the appointment of a relatively inexperienced player to the captaincy, possibly ahead of those whose seniority have given them an influential place in the club's scheme of things, can lead to an excessive reliance on support from certain quarters of the administration. The seniority of the appointee can dictate the extent to which he is able to assume by right the authority his role should presuppose; a player who has gained respect through long standing in both the team and the club should have little difficulty in asserting command, certainly at first. Where the committee contains a figure of outstanding stature – Brian Close in Yorkshire is an obvious example, although it would be unfair to suggest that administrative problems are exclusive to that county alone – the new captain, especially if inexperienced, can find his position particularly compromised.

The responsibility of the captain is to state in advance the terms upon which he will accept the job; it is an obligation he cannot evade if he is to bring into focus the uncertain relations of power that exist in the club. It is not a matter of arrogance but of foresight; by the inherent potential for instability in the hierarchy, confusion and even contention will replace direction if the captain fails to demand full control. Mike Gatting at Middlesex, for example, while taking sincere heed of the coaching staff and cricket committee, would always have the final say in cricket matters. If this was a right won by the talents and efforts of Mike Brearley before him, it is nonetheless one upon which Gatting will have insisted when accepting the invitation to lead the county.

For the captain certainly, and to a lesser, perhaps dangerously inadequate degree, for all the playing staff, there are relationships outside the squad which also have an important influence. 'Above' the captain (although such indications of rank are rather ambiguous here) are the committee and the secretary. The general workings of the committee in most of its subsidiary areas are not usually seen as directly relevant to the player's future, and the sub-committees which oversee the development of club and ground, the county's financial dealings, the employment of non-playing staff and so on should ideally run parallel to, but distinct from, the body which concerns itself with cricket. It is this group, usually termed the cricket committee, which exercises significant power over the players by helping to formulate cricketing strategies and determine careers. The man standing between the committee and the players and acting as a conduit for decisions from 'above' and for responses and opinions from 'below', is the secretary.

Cricket committees characteristically comprise four or so members of the wider club committee who have been elected or appointed by that body, plus the captain and one or more of coach, cricket manager (if the post exists) and vice-captain. Formally, the professional element in the committee is there in an advisory capacity, although, as we have seen, it is incumbent on the captain himself to insist that his desires and ideas are in most instances adhered to. More recently, some counties have begun to streamline the structure, and cricket has been put in the hands of the professional core (captain, vice-captain, coach and/or cricket manager) with one or two members of the committee attending meetings to establish liaison and report on the desires of the cricket leadership back to the full executive. If we can assume that relations within the club's administration are reasonably harmonious and that the captain is not forever thwarted in his plans by contradictory strategies from 'above' (a too hopeful assumption, sometimes), it might well be wondered – and often is, by the players – what precisely the committee member contributes. Yet a captain can gain a great deal from members of a cricket committee, especially from its chairman with whom he can forge, in the best of circumstances, a highly productive alliance.

Again, to speak in ideal terms, the chairman might be a respected figure from the county's past (the further removed from contemporary cricket the better, perhaps, though this is not always true) who can support and guide the captain from the perspective of a longstanding but detached presence in the game. Such a chairman observes cricket frequently enough, but the quality of his advice, on matters of group motivation, conditions of employment or problems with certain individuals, will derive from his wide experience of essentially non-cricketing matters. He is a source not of tactical insight, then, but of quiet wisdom who can sometimes appreciate a problem precisely because he is remote from it. Cricketers too often forget that they are playing a game whose outcome is determined at least as much by attitude and psychology as by technical prowess: familiarity with life can hardly be a disadvantage.

If this picture of a benign grey eminence would be derided as Utopian by many a professional cricketer, his own characteristic parody of the typical committeeman is surely equally unsound. The cricketer's distrust of committees is historic and probably intrinsic to the very idea of amateur administrators deciding the fate of professional players. The professional doubts the amateur's commitment of time and effort and believes that their respective contributions to the club are laughably unequal.

Although a captain should certainly advise on who is to be retained on a county staff and on the types of contract to be offered, these decisions are in the last instance more fairly, and thus perhaps better, made by someone detached from the dressing-room. Somebody must be able to overrule a captain with regard to personnel to ensure that closeness to the team and personal preferences and antipathies do not prejudice the decision. The professional might argue that amateurs are not competent to make that judgement, but these amateurs are, if nothing else, democratically elected by the club's membership and subject to motions of no confidence at a general meeting. If these amateurs are truly inept, then so is the whole structure of county organisation as it has come down to us; the need is for those concerned, including cricketers themselves, to propose new ways of proceeding. This assessment may do little more than invite Orwell's critique of Dickens that, in the end, it says no more than 'if only people could be a little more decent to one another, everything would be fine.' Yet the problems which arise from the player's cautious resentment of the committeeman might be greatly overcome if both parties took more interest in each other as individuals.

The professional cricketer can be woefully cocooned and ostrich-like in his attitude to the world off the field; he could himself make far greater efforts to know committeemen both professionally and socially. Ultimately, however, the problem is structural and requires somebody in the club – the secretary, most obviously – to put in place the means by which the two sides are brought regularly together. Half an hour of drinks every fortnight is not enough for committee members to understand the ways of a cricketer's mind; nor, indeed, for cricketers to discover respect for individuals who, by and large, have the sincere interests of their club at heart.

Although a committee's decision can bring to an end a professional cricketer's career (the euphemism is that the player has been 'released', of course, as though he were a serf or convict), it is important to realise that the relationship is not in any ordinary sense one of employer to employee. The club's officers do not make money out of the labour of the players; counties themselves seek only to break even, and such profits as are made are devoted to the further well-being and expansion of the club. Unquestionably greater energy could be devoted to the welfare of cricketers, and a committee's sense of priorities is invariably debatable. In theory, however, and usually in practice, both sides have a genuinely common aim – the playing success of the team. Since this aim would be vastly better served by an equally common sense of purpose and identity, and a greater feeling of security for the player, it is astonishing how few clubs have sought ways of assuring a continuing and productive interchange between professional and amateur.

The trend, however, albeit a painfully slow one, has indeed been towards the greater involvement of the players. If cricketers' views only filter through the captain and coach to the cricket committee and, in a further diluted form, thence to the general committee, these views are becoming increasingly respected. It has never been the case that players have sought a direct, collective role in the higher levels of decision-making, either through internal club organisation or through the general initiative of the Cricketers' Association. The Association has gained representation within the overall structure of the TCCB – with places on, for example, the cricket, discipline and registration committees – but at club level innovations have remained the prerogative of the individual.

Certain developments here are worth noting. Ian Greig, in establishing the terms of his remit on taking the Surrey captaincy, clearly saw his role as extending well beyond the field of play: in moving into a position of considerable influence both in the club's cricket and in its commercial policy, he has taken a player's perspective deep into the fabric of the Oval. At Worcester Duncan Fearnley's efforts as club chairman to integrate the worlds of dressing-room and committee room have bred a sense of confidence in the staff which has been instrumental, however obliquely, in their on-field success.

There have been appreciable shifts of emphasis, then, and the pace of change, by competitive necessity, has certainly quickened throughout the late 1980s. Yet it should be admitted that the majority of players would still retain a mostly unqualified sympathy for the remarks of Bob Cottam, Warwickshire's cricket manager, on resigning from that county in 1990. Cottam reportedly observed: 'It has been like trying to do a job with handcuffs on. The point about the cricket committee is that, if these people saw enough cricket, you could appreciate their opinions. One member of the committee saw only half a day's play last season, yet he gets the same vote as me.'

Without specific analysis of Warwickshire's problems it would be invidious to take sides in that particular dispute. The issue is further confused by Cottam's very role as cricket manager, a post whose place in the administrative order has still not been resolved. To state the obvious, however, definitions of power and responsibility at Edgbaston had evidently fallen apart badly. The modest point is that county structures have an in-built tendency towards such dislocation unless real efforts, conscious and unconscious, social and professional, are made to promote cohesion.

The figure to whom this unenviable task will frequently devolve in the organisation is the paid secretary or chief executive. His is the post (and, in the light of developments in comparable areas of business and industry, it is worth saying that there had never been a female secretary before Lancashire's Rose Fitzgibbon in 1991) which demands greatest flexibility and sensitivity to the changing needs of the club. The tone of his involvement can alter as swiftly as the composition of either team or committee – literally overnight in the case of a secretary who sees a new cricket committee voted into place or a new general committee elected at an AGM. In one regime the secretary may have to assume a forceful, initiating presence, taking a prominent part in cricketing or contractual matters; in another it may be politic to proceed diplomatically and cultivate a mediating, back-seat influence.

It falls on the secretary, in short, to hold the balance in a club. If he does the job well, his intermediary function will extend not simply to the relationship between players and committee; the secretary should also ensure that the potentially antagonistic concerns of the club's commercial, administrative and playing wings are regulated by an overall strategy. It need hardly be observed that this is a job description more readily expressed than fulfilled. Although the secretary's contribution is so important, he is not assisted by the general truth in cricket that all decision-making is far too slow. From the International Cricket Conference through the committees of the TCCB to the workings of a county club, deliberation and implementation is a ponderous process. For the most part, secretaries cannot make decisions swiftly and unilaterally enough. They are bound to await the ratification of a monthly committee meeting which may not be fully attended or which lacks the presence of an individual central to the subject under debate.

Since the clubs are themselves not always sure where power lies or should lie, and who has the ability to exercise what areas of authority, the problem is further compounded. If this indeterminate set of relations makes the influence of certain forceful individuals more decisive than it is in other hierarchies, the secretary himself is impeded by his formal status as an employee of the club, a paid administrator rather than a director of policy. As his position is, to a degree, only tenable to the extent that he can retain the confidence of players to the one side and committees to the other, the temptation will be to avoid substantive action for fear he might upset either party.

If the secretary is expected to have his finger on the pulse of the club, it would be a helpful development if more immediate, executive power could pass to him, certainly in the absence of other individuals prepared to accept responsibility. This would be especially pertinent in matters of winter employment for the players, to give one of many examples. Here his involvement in the daily running of the club presents frequent opportunities to initiate schemes whose realisation is hindered by the need to refer back to the bureaucracy. In matters of discipline, too, a secretary's inability to make swift and credible judgements will harm the club by allowing ostensibly minor grievances to expand into sources of internal strife. As the public face of the committee, the person who on the basis of almost daily contact is expected to communicate to the players the tenor of the committee's thinking and help to ensure that the efforts of both sides are in fact unified, the secretary clearly has to enjoy a degree of trust. It is by no means easy for this to be established if the belief persists that the secretary lacks any real consequence in the club's operations, or if it is felt that his attention to the players' arguments is merely symbolic.

Into these obscure, even arcane levels of cricket organisation there has developed a recent inclination to insert yet another layer of authority: the cricket manager. Part of the responsibility to bridge the divide which separates team from committee should now pass to him, and his formal standing will either be somewhere between the captain and the team or between captain and secretary. A further possibility is that captain and manager form a single bloc to deal directly with the committee, relegating the secretary to a purely administrative capacity. Again the posture is ill-defined, as so often in the hierarchy of a club.

It is important here to distinguish the role of manager at Test level from the post being created in the counties, in spite of the common terminology. The England manager – Micky Stewart in 1991 – has a wide remit which entails, ultimately, the overseeing and construction of cricket's entire pyramid of development so that it will yield the best pool of talent for the England squad. He is far better placed than any captain to gauge the general texture of first-class cricket outside the confines of a single county.

Within a county, however, where the playing staff will rarely number more than twenty-five, the need for a manager is much less apparent. Rather than ask what need there should be for the employment of another element in the leadership, the tendency has been to add a new ingredient to the mixture and hope it will resolve problems which themselves remain unidentified. Self-examination is replaced by one more character (of considerable standing in the game, usually) in search of a role. Thus the counties are accepting that the present office-holders have failed to complete their briefs in full, and they are doing so without asking whether or not the organisation of the clubs was in fact responsible for that failure. If a new addition was to be made to the staffs of clubs who so often plead poverty, it would surely most beneficially relate to off-season activities. As managers have been installed, however, they have taken a job that could – and arguably should – be done by a combination of the captain, secretary and coach.

Behind this ostensible superfluity there is an unspoken and often unconscious recognition that domestic cricket has become decidedly complex. To look at the role of a successful cricket manager, Ken Taylor at Nottinghamshire, who assisted the club's development for a long period prior to the present wave of new appointments, his role had a very definite direction.

Taylor observed the decision-making at Trent Bridge at all levels and became a unifying factor, assuming, in effect, part of the responsibilities of the secretary and allowing the actual secretary to become an administrator. The development of Nottinghamshire's cricketing future, especially after the club had shown the wisdom to appoint so able a figure as Clive Rice to the captaincy, proceeded under Taylor's influence in an efficient, organised and purposeful way. This was well illustrated in the subsequent choice of West Indian all-round Franklyn Stephenson to take the position of single overseas player in succession to the irreplaceable pairing of Rice and Richard Hadlee. Management here entailed the discussion of the club's precise playing needs in the context of their existing team resources and the selection of a player as much for his character and attitude as for his ability. It was a careful and considered process of matching a man to a club, using an understanding that had only been built up through long and astute association. More to the point, it was the decision of an off-the-field participant; it had never been Taylor's role to engage in any of the team's concerns once it had left the pavilion.

This is not true of the 1991 grouping of tracksuit managers, such as Gloucestershire's Eddie Barlow, Northamptonshire's Mike Procter and Leicestershire's Bobby Simpson, who organise training, administer the team's daily practical arrangements and seek a personal understanding of a player's make-up. This last role is significantly new and takes on part of the function both of captain and of the old senior professional. The cricket manager becomes an ear to talk to, a man who can hear different points of view and attempt to synthesise them, one who seeks to explain to players their role in a team and reconcile them to it. He is, then, a conciliator and, in that he presumably enjoys close harmony with the captain, he is a man through whom disagreement can be suggested and concern expressed. The putative need for such a figure is not because, as might be first supposed, captains now have less time at their disposal for a broadly paternal role; it is because the requirements of players themselves have changed. A cricketer's ambition, frustration and sensitivity is now altogether more intense than even fifteen years ago; where once a player was, in the main, content to continue season by season, contributing fully and anticipating that this would bring another contract at the summer's end, he is now significantly more eager to express himself.

Those few outsiders who, for whatever reason, are lucky enough to be accepted into close proximity to a county staff are very often taken aback by the extent of the insecurity which can be found; it is also surprising, even alarming, to note how limited are the occasions when cricketers feel able to discuss amongst themselves the real origins of their disquiet. The reasons for this are undoubtedly social as much as cricketing. Since the tendency towards dislocation and breakdown in all walks of life has lent such novel prominence to consultative and counselling services, it is perhaps not so surprising that cricket fails to be an untroubled escape. Indeed, it can be argued that the pressure of the number of different competitions today, with an attendant powerful demand for success in at least one, and the increasing gulf in financial rewards between Test and county cricket have brought entirely new anxieties into the game itself.

Certainly the contemporary cricketer has a heightened regard both for his place in the club's medium-term thinking and for his status and his future. There is, moreover, a greater readiness to give voice to ambition at an earlier age, and the old professional, nurtured in a different era, will sometimes grumble about a younger player that, 'He should worry more about his own game and forget things that don't concern him'. The resentment present in this attitude is misplaced, for the new urgency to achieve success and contribute to the development of a side can be creative and beneficial. Yet the implied gulf between senior and junior players has placed a strain on the inherited structures of authority in certain clubs, and so the cricket manager can be seen to fulfil the now mainly defunct role of senior professional.

The place of the coach in such reorganised regimes has become uncertain. At the level of the Second XI, helping players up to the age of perhaps 19 or 20, the good coach exerts both a technical influence and a counselling one. At the higher, first-team level his cricketing input has less to do with formal coaching than with continually stressing to players why they are good at the game and where they have slipped from their own best standards. Although this has clearly become at least part of the manager's function, there is in his appointment a tacit expectation that he is to offer more than the traditional coach.

It is as if the changed character of the professional game, and the altered priorities within it, are being conceded in practice before they are addressed in theory. The supposed answer, a cricket manager, is thrown at a problem which has not itself been defined. It is also perhaps fair, if a little sad, to observe that a captain's historical allies, his vice-captain and senior colleagues, can no longer always be relied upon to provide selfless assistance; the self-interest and ambition we have noted is not restricted to eager youngsters alone.

Let us avoid overstatement. Throughout the last five years the movement in county cricket has been towards a streamlining of levels of effective power and, by implication, towards a reduction in the committee ranks of those seeking prominence for reasons of local kudos rather than from a genuine commitment to the progress of a club. Whether the recent vogue for the role of middle-man will in fact prove counter to this search for purposeful management, only succeeding summers will reveal. It needs to be repeated, the more so in relation to the changing character of county cricket discussed above, that the key individual in successful organisation should still be the captain. The strong captain will continue to set his own terms of reference and, if a manager is to be part of the structure, it will be for the captain to establish exactly how he is best employed.

Different personalities working within different regimes will seek different divisions of responsibility; good captains will seek a chemistry they can control and direct towards success. What a captain cannot allow, if he is to hope for any progress, is a degree of disengagement from his players which prevents his philosophy being plainly understood. Whatever the sensibility of the contemporary player and whatever the form of a club's organisation, if the captain fails to provide the team's sense of direction it will emerge from no other source.

Followers of the game sometimes entertain the pleasingly romantic hope that there is a certain individual aura to any particular county's cricket, an atmosphere which endures through changes of personnel or policy. It is a notion rooted perhaps in the rural origins of the game and in the times when England contained significantly distinct regional identities; the existence of genuinely local cultures and economies and the physical remoteness of one community from another might once have lent a certain mystique to the visit of a team from Lancashire or Nottingham, say, to Horsham or Basingstoke. Except in matters of the merest peripheral detail this is no longer the case, attractive though the illusion remains. The causes of this transformation belong to the process of post-war history rather than to cricket, although the game can offer trends of its own. Staffs are now increasingly transient, meaning that there is no longer a definite 'feel' to a county eleven. In any season today some twenty or so cricketers will turn out for a new county; that is, excluding débutants, about 5 per cent of those appearing in the Championship each year have played for a different team the season before.

Even where this is not ostensibly a major factor (in the case of Yorkshire, for example), the common imperatives of county cricket – success through commercial solvency, fitness, bowling points and one-day all-rounders – impart a certain uniformity and dictate a break with the past. If one has an image of how a team plays or of the general outlook it will display on the field, what used to be traditional county characteristics fail to hold up. Derbyshire is no longer a collection of inveterate grafters and mean seamers; Yorkshiremen no longer bring a technical presence to their game which is somehow particular to them. There is a case to be made for differences in mentality between individual cricketers, but these are differences of class and education rather than of regional identity.

Direction, then, comes not from history or local custom but from captaincy and the organisational assistance a captain enjoys. The most telling support for this contention comes from Essex, although followers of Middlesex will argue that their county has found an equally successful formula. The recent record of Essex is so impressive that devotees of the Championship under the age of 25 could be forgiven the entirely false impression that the 'Essex way' has been a permanent feature of cricket's evolution.

Between 1978 and 1990, Essex only three times ended the season lower than fifth in the table; after 1983 they failed to finish in the top four just once. Yet for most of the 1970s, the team was viewed by opponents as dour and cheerless in the extreme, and a visit to the rustic dilapidation of Chelmsford was the low point of a season. The county staff comprised fourteen players, and the club endured a reputation for the precise opposite of the camaraderie and affability with which it is always now associated. The 'Essex way', in other words, was a creation of the last fifteen years.

The image of Essex as a side who not only win, but win in a relaxed, sometimes almost antic, spirit of self-belief has grown from squads assembled first under Brian Taylor and then, more notably, under Keith Fletcher. The key decision of the committee was to appoint each of these men to the captaincy, men who by no stretch of the imagination filled the stereotyped profile of the classic amateur leader still so beloved in certain quarters of the game. Having made the choice, the administration then displayed the strength of its own convictions and gave the captain a freedom to formulate and impress his own philosophy. Once success had been gained on a consistent basis it was altogether more easy for Essex sides to sustain their excellent attitude to the game: good humour and mutual respect come more readily with victory than with defeat. Yet there has been no complacency about Essex, and for all the clowning which so endeared Ray East or John Lever to the county's followers there has been a purpose and a tenacity to the team which flowed both from Fletcher's own approach and from his eye for the right man to elevate to prominence.

The point is worth stressing. Many cricketers are guilty of an almost fatalistic reverence for success as though its properties were both magical and automatically self-perpetuating. Of the nucleus of the first sides to start winning under Fletcher, only Graham Gooch remained in 1990; Neil Foster and Derek Pringle were later additions. The attitude for which the team is famous has therefore been renewed season by season and persists by virtue of a level of expectation which is now almost part of the very structure of the club. The continuing ability to win is not a matter of incantation, then, but of effort and of foresight in the club's organisation: Essex sides seem always to have a fine blend of age groups, the embryo of the next first team apparent years in advance. Contrary to the myth, success does not of itself breed success. For fifteen years prior to the end of the 1970s, Kent enjoyed a period of eminence as seemingly inviolable as that of Essex thereafter; their subsequent decline owed a great deal to precisely those errors, confusions and inconsistencies of management outlined above.

The example of Kent helps correct the impression which may be gained of a slow shift in cricket power towards the wealth of the South-East. On the face of it the long-term supremacy of Essex and Middlesex argues for this, as did the relative achievement of Sussex, traditionally one of the weaker sides, for seven years into the mid-1980s. In each case, however, captaincy provides the common theme: Taylor and then Fletcher at Essex, Mike Brearley and Mike Gatting at Middlesex, and the greatly underrated John Barclay at Hove. Moreover, some of the attention in recent seasons has begun to turn northwards again.

The recent success of Lancashire possibly makes the point about captaincy more forcibly than any other. The county's administration can be criticised for an affection for the one-day game which is occasionally to the detriment of Lancashire's Championship challenge, but in the appointment of David Hughes, complemented perfectly by Alan Ormrod as coach and organiser of cricket at junior levels, they showed remarkable courage. Hughes was the nearest thing to what had appeared an impossibility in the modern game: the non-playing captain. He led a side as notable as most for the number of wilful and forthcoming individuals it contained, yet despite his somewhat limited contribution of runs and wickets (Hughes's fielding remained outstanding) he and Ormrod began to make Lancashire's undoubted talent at last do justice to itself.

The question which may arise here is, 'Can you take a short cut and fabricate a successful cricket team?' If the Essex experience is not fully relevant, in that most of the players moulded by Taylor and Fletcher were home-grown, the obvious case study is Worcestershire. The Worcester administration brings together many of the strands so far discussed: in Duncan

Fearnley they have a forceful, very public chairman committed to finding a medium-term strategy for the county; Phil Neale is an intelligent, quietly astute captain, greatly removed in temperament and character from his chairman but equally aware of the need for planning; Tim Curtis is tactically an immensely able vice-captain working closely and unobtrusively with Neale; Mike Vockins is a supremely discreet secretary, exactly suited to the role of intermediary in a club with highly prominent personalities on both sides.

Between 1975 and 1984 Worcestershire avoided a double-figure Championship placing only once, their worse run since the 1930s. From this legacy of failure, a process of self-examination embraced first an assessment of their home grounds and then of the playing resources required in those conditions to bring balance to the squad. As the overseas player, a batsman of the highest quality was chosen to ensure a consistent source of reliable runs and, to complement Phil Newport, two bowlers, Neal Radford and later Graham Dilley, were signed to form the core of a very strong side. The even more celebrated recruitment of Ian Botham in 1987 ironically proved less influential in the change at Worcester due to persistent cruel luck with injury.

One is tempted to say that the rest is history. Yet the fact that Worcestershire should, in five of the next six seasons, finish in the top five conceals more than it reveals. Those in the game who have rather resented their success, implying that it has been bought, ignore the fact that signings alone cannot guarantee triumph. The requirement is still for good leadership and for sound judgement, and the club must be confident in the ability of its organisation to draw the best out of newcomers. Dilley and Botham arrived, after all, following bitter disagreement with Kent and Somerset respectively; Radford had spent five largely unproductive seasons with Lancashire; and Graeme Hick was only 18 years old when he made his Worcestershire début. The real evidence that there is far more to the building of a team than making highly publicised signings emerged in 1989 when, with the eleven totally depleted by injury, Worcestershire won nine out of twelve games in July and August to retain the Championship. It was a momentum sustained, in the main, by two unheralded fast bowlers, Steve McEwan and

Stuart Lampitt, who at the season's start had only forty-four first-class appearances between them.

It may arguably be true that a one-off, instant success could be contrived by the sudden injection into the Championship of a side of major signings, but continuous achievement requires that the right attitude has been nurtured throughout the staff. For those that fear the development of a transfer system in cricket, and the ability of rich clubs to monopolise the game's domestic honours, the TCCB's regulations now prevent this becoming an easy process. Clubs can sign only one player per season whose registration has been contested by his former county, and only two such players in a five-year period. Of far greater relevance, however, is the actual experience of Essex again.

When Northamptonshire visited Chelmsford in 1990, David Ripley, the county's highly perceptive wicket-keeper, engaged slow left-armer John Childs in a discussion with which the Essex players must have become all too familiar. Ripley asked whether Childs could perhaps highlight one element above all others which revealed the Essex secret. Childs, a typically sage Essex signing when released after ten seasons with Gloucestershire, could put his finger on no single factor other than the county's pay structure. It was perhaps the fact, he said, that each player knew what all his team-mates earned, that there were open, fixed scales of reward related to seniority and status, and nobody was above this. Here is one further indication of an administration which has thought very carefully about how to create the conditions for success. It is not a coincidence that neither Essex nor Middlesex have signed any of the prime, contested players who have sought to change counties in recent years.

There is a final figure in the workings of a club who was once all but unknown, and the idea that part of a county's precious and limited financial resources could be devoted to the employment of a commercial or promotions manager belongs to the last fifteen years at most. Yet the raising of revenue independent of gate receipts or membership fees has now become so integral to the well-being of county cricket that there is a genuine danger of financial considerations harming the interests of the game itself. Most instances of this are well rehearsed and require only a passing note here.

When club committees discuss proposals for change and instruct their chairman on how to vote within the TCCB, they invariably claim, and often spell out, purely cricketing grounds for their decisions. If it is as well to record that fact it would be only honest to add that very few players believe the accompanying denials of an overriding commercial motive. Thus, although their own cricket committees might recommend a Championship comprised of four-day games – and 80 per cent of players would endorse that – clubs retain the status quo and allege that they do so for the good of the game. This lacks conviction.

It would be true to say that among the playing staffs of most counties there is a deep dislike of Sunday League cricket. In itself this need not command any privileged attention: the mere preferences of cricketers do not necessarily carry a relevance to the game's wider debates. When, however, the great majority of players would go on to insist – as has indeed been insisted by both the England management and specifically convened commissions of inquiry – that 40-over cricket does positive harm to levels of skill in the English game, there is a considerable argument for change. Yet the counties refuse to disturb the lucrative framework of eight home Sunday League fixtures, with their assurance of established rewards in sponsorship, advertising and the sale of hospitality boxes, because, they argue, budgets could not be balanced otherwise. Even the pretence of a non-commercial logic is abandoned here, and advocates of an amendment to the programme are, in turn, reduced to financial pleading: if England's international standing declines, then gates at Test matches fall and the counties' share of the profits diminishes.

When the primacy of commercial interests seems to compromise not only the game's basic skills but also its very meaning, it is as well, perhaps, to pose fundamental questions. Counties imply that they need the present formats of one-day and Championship cricket to sustain their current levels of expenditure. Players cannot have it both ways, it is argued: if they seek better rewards they must accept types of cricket which generate income. Quite apart from the suspicion here that committees are too complacently side-stepping the need to find fresh sources of funding, the essential theme should surely concern the purpose county clubs are supposed to serve.

If professional cricket is not to be played for reasons which derive from the worth of the game itself, why should it be played at all? The ultimate logic of deferring solely to a club's preservation and expansion, as though this were a sufficient aim in itself, is that anything may be done to make money. By this rationale we would be as well to seek a constant provision of ever more instant forms of cricket, and the central question – what exactly are we trying to preserve? – is lost. Unless the purpose of a county cricket club points to something greater than itself, to the value of playing a game with a coherent history and identity to the highest standard, it has no meaning beyond self-perpetuation.

There is another indirectly related area of the sociology of the game which cricket has addressed all too rarely. Only recently has it been realised, with considerable alarm, that the game's social base has narrowed dangerously, and efforts are at last being made to face the problem of cricket's near-disappearance in state education. What are the backgrounds of professional cricketers and how do they influence play?

Even the most cursory investigation of where contemporary professionals were educated unearths some quite astonishing facts. In the space of two years the same school, Willesden High in North-West London, turned out two cricketers, Phillip DeFreitas and Chris Lewis, who played for England in their early 20s. In the 1990 season three men under the age of 25, with a space of five years (or one school 'turn-over') between them, played Championship cricket for three separate counties; the common factor for Gareth Smith (Warwickshire), Simon Brown (Northamptonshire) and Martin Thursfield (then Middlesex, now Hampshire) was that all attended Boldon Comprehensive in Sunderland. In five years, then, just two state secondary schools produced five first-class cricketers, of whom two went on to gain Test honours and one, Brown, to represent Young England.

Cricket is obviously alive and thriving in these schools, and there are members of staff keen to provide children with the opportunity to play. The point, of course, is that a generation ago this was the case throughout education, and it is a measure of how widely cricket has disappeared from the sporting curriculum that one is surprised to find, not that the game is being promoted in these two schools, but that it is being played at all. It is hard to avoid the fear that perhaps hundreds of cricketers of a potentially first-class standard have been lost for the want of a wider educational base to the game.

That conclusion is prompted yet more forcibly by the experience of the Haringey Cricket College. This was established under a scheme funded by the local authority to provide both training in cricket and further education for unemployed youths drawn essentially from a single London borough. The results of this project have been remarkable: in six years, seven graduates of the scheme have played county cricket. It is immaterial to argue that some of these cricketers have failed to secure a prominent place in professional squads (although in the cases of Gloucestershire's Mark Alleyne and Warwickshire's Keith Piper there is sufficient ability to suggest long-term futures), for this would be true of the majority of trialists. While one or two of these players might perhaps have found other routes into the game, most would have remained completely unknown; of how many others, one wonders, has this been true? The bulk of the college's entrants were educated within five miles of Tottenham; if a solitary inner-city project can prove so productive, what might result from an expansion of such opportunities to even a handful of other towns?

It is certainly the case that privately educated cricketers are now far more prevalent in the professional game than they were twenty years ago. Sadly it also seems to be the case that we will not return to the norm of the 1950s and early 1960s when the regular group coaching of cricket was a feature of games lessons in secondary education summer by summer. If the 1944 Education Act stipulates that the teaching of PE is mandatory, it does not prescribe which sport should be nurtured: schools are required today to consider 'cost effectiveness', and cricket needs space, groundsmanship and relatively expensive kit.

The recent questioning of standards of play at the highest levels of the professional game have thankfully worried cricket authorities sufficiently to prompt belated action. Various initiatives have latterly emerged from the TCCB which have given the National Cricket Association, with its admirable network of professional and amateur support, a prominence it should arguably have been granted more than a decade ago. One hopes that a crisis which remained unacknowledged for far too long may perhaps now have passed. There is a pertinent difference, however, between making cricket available to all who seek it out and implanting the game in the national culture through exposure at school.

If the idea of a regional 'feel' to a county, in so far as it can be imparted by geography, is untenable, does the social background of a player, and in some instances of a team, nonetheless lend a discernible difference to play? Generalisation risks contributing to cricket's abundant stock of myth; it is judicious, then, to begin with facts. The following are the approximate ratios of state-educated to privately educated players on respective county staffs: Kent 2:1 ; Hampshire 3:1 ; Northamptonshire 6:1. The Somerset ratio is 1:1, but here the local influence of Millfield School, with its emphasis on sport and bursaries for those gifted at cricket, distorts the picture. Do such statistics have a bearing? What distinctions, if any, can be detected between the approaches of Northamptonshire and those of Hampshire and Kent?

A Kent or Hampshire team typically conveys what might be called collective confidence. Where Northamptonshire cricketers have confidence in their own abilities as individuals, this is not necessarily reflected in the attitude of the unit. In consequence, on suffering a bad defeat or losing a game that should have been drawn, the side will often fail to pull itself round sufficiently quickly. When confronting the set-back, then, there is the tendency to allow the trough of disappointment to last too long and affect performance in the following match. A Kent eleven, however, rarely betrays such uncertainty. An apparently inherent confidence in themselves and each other enables them, on the surface at least, to bounce back from defeat; a collection of Kent cricketers leave a club car park after a disappointing game without the same degree of evident depression and brooding you would associate with a working-class team.

The composure revealed in such minor detail is not a question of technical differences; it is not a result of more intensive coaching at school, for example. Such assurance is drawn from

76

the cricketer's wider social background. In a purely material sense, less anxiety and pressure afflicts a man who does not feel that his life is wedded to continuing success as a cricketer alone. More than this, a player who has long devoted himself to the single-minded pursuit of a career in the game is prone to an introspection which is not always beneficial to his cricket. Since the game as a whole is a developing series of separate match situations, it is perhaps more open to the broader perspective: personal dedication by itself cannot alter the performance of a team. If a side can calmly learn the lessons of defeat, it enjoys a great asset if it can begin a new match regardless of yesterday's failure.

There are obvious qualifications to this argument; self-assurance and detachment are no guarantee of the advantage. Hampshire, for example, despite their impressive playing resources persistently fell short of their potential throughout the 1980s, although they had no shortage of confidence. By contrast, the Middlesex team, in social terms a slice of lower middle-class North London, has cultivated such a depth of self-belief from its recent tradition of success that it quickly inspires the newcomer with a formidable will to win. The generalisation retains this degree of truth, however; if a side with Northamptonshire's talent could ally its ability to the outlook of Kent it would not be so prone to the loss of collective nerve which so besets its cricket.

The proposition might be more clearly advanced on an individual level. Peter Willey and David Gower are Test players who captained Leicestershire in successive seasons. Each attracted equally simplistic complaint, the one for being too sternly committed, the other for being not committed enough. The background of these cricketers is hugely significant. Willey, the boy from County Durham who made his first-class début at the age of 16, is almost the archetypal working-class professional. The first player at the ground every morning, he prepares himself rigorously; on the field he gives everything, off it he looks after himself almost obsessively. There is just a hint in this ethic of something approaching tragedy: when cricket ends, what exactly replaces it? For David Gower there is a pride in performance which is just as deep as Willey's but not so devoted to method. It is his misfortune to believe that, because it is only natural to be disappointed with failure, he does not need to dwell on or express that disappointment; he was born almost as inevitably in Tunbridge Wells as he was left-handed. The fluency of his batting comes from knowing a world beyond the crease, and his frailty perhaps suggests that he knows this too well.

Willey came into cricket without knowing anything else. Gower, though he stayed at King's School, Canterbury, to achieve a place at university, left higher education to play cricket at 18. They share at least that contrast, then, to the more familiar professional cricketer of today, the player who, with the cushion of qualifications, still consciously opts for a cricketing career. The wisdom of this approach has been increasingly urged by the counties which, for the most part, support those younger professionals who seek further education. In a way, this is the ideal social preparation.

Quite apart from the practical benefit of gaining insurance against injury or failure, a certain awareness of life enhances a player's understanding both of his own game and of the problems of team expression. The age of 22 or 23 is an excellent time to address professional cricket. By choosing this path before available alternatives, a player will usually say much about his motivation and attitude; any lost technical ground can be made up almost by the very receptivity and discrimination which has been developed outside the game. If there is a model of adequate preparation to be suggested to the would-be professional, it perhaps lies here.

A vast association of factors underpins the ability of a professional cricket team to reach its highest fulfilment. Since the criterion of success, victory on the field, is so implacably unambiguous, most must settle for the struggle rather than the prize. In these opening chapters we have considered talent, attitude, balance, organisation and, in its widest sense, a team's prevailing culture. The list is not complete and, alas, the problem is probably falsified by the neat divisions of discussion: ultimately cricket is played, realised in practice, not reduced to theories. What precedes play is unquestionably critical; what is witnessed, however, is the game itself.

FOUR

Championship Cricket

We should begin, perhaps, with the game's own principal player: the pitch. Cricket is unique among ball games in its relationship with the physical world; certainly when played in its authentic, longer forms, it provides a constant interaction between a player's skill and the results of climate and nature. Some discussions at a match, with their references to soil types and growth of grass, relative humidity and water tables, appear to belong more to horticulture than to entertainment. Thus the debate provoked by the decision to cover pitches and end their exposure to rainfall was not simply an argument about the role of spinners; it was as if the very essence of the game was being affronted by commercialism and by an alien desire for conformity. It seemed to point away from a past in which cricketers performed in the ever-changing conditions of an English summer and towards a future of artificial, uniform surfaces and anonymous settings.

Because a Championship campaign lasts for some five months and embraces diverse venues around the country, a key element in individual and team success remains the ability to adapt; a player adapts both to different pitches and to the different types of match which they produce. Despite the unacceptable predictability which various codes of pitch preparation encouraged in the late 1980s, first-class cricket is still a game which is scheduled to last for at least nineteen hours. Even where the pitch is woefully bland and sterile – which is to say it lacks bounce, speed and any hint of movement for either fast or slow bowler – the character of a game's evolution over these nineteen hours will be underpinned by the pitch. Although this is far less true of a one-day game, the pitch's pace will dictate what is a reasonable score in the overs available and early moisture, for example, can assist the side fielding first.

There is, however, a need to be clear about the precise influence a pitch exerts. Despite sometimes fatalistic claims to the contrary, the outcome of a match is not predestined by conditions, but is dependent upon the attitudes and abilities of the players who must marry their cricket to a context. The pitch establishes the tone of a match; it does not dictate who wins it.

Although it is true, for example, that if one team's best efforts can achieve only 250 runs, the opposition should never be able to blaze their way to 500, it is not the case that greater skill and an earlier reading of conditions will be denied their reward. Only those surfaces upon which a ball landing in approximately the same place might do one of a number of wholly unpredictable things can be said to reduce a match to little more than luck – and surfaces like that were a rarity even at the height of the pitch controversy in the late 1980s. Equally, those pitches which are rightly described as 'too good' for a three-day game can be countered – albeit in too limited a way, perhaps – by greater subtlety and accuracy from a bowler and increased initiative and enterprise from captains.

The question of adaptability may well crystallise for players into the difference between typical home pitches and those found elsewhere. In the 1970s and early 1980s, Northampton offered very slow surfaces which occasionally provided a degree of help to the seamers but were in general turgid and lacking in bounce. In consequence, batsmen often became front-foot thrusters for whom stroke-play on the back foot was a dangerous indulgence even where possible. The player who pre-eminently made a virtue of these limitations was David Steele, who successfully carried his defensive skills and patient front-foot method into Test matches in which, while all about him bowed to pace, he kept at bay the Australian and West Indian attacks in 1975 and 1976. While Steele applied a temperament nurtured on slow pitches so well as to achieve almost folk-hero status, more restricted players like Brian Crump effectively carved out professional county careers for themselves as bits-and-pieces cricketers. These were men who could bowl flat, squat seamers to just short of a length and survive in the middle order by moving steadfastly on to the front foot.

Such pitches were common at many county headquarters in the Midlands where tired clay soils, subject to up to 100 years of intensive use at Derby, Leicester or Edgbaston, made for a preponderance of home draws and the difficulty of ever securing enough results to win the Championship. It is a problem which has to a degree now confronted groundsmen throughout the country – Canterbury, for example, has become a typically slow and bounceless pitch – and many have made manful strides to inject pace by digging up squares and relaying with 'foreign' soils in depth.

For batsmen whose ability and inclinations led them to try to score rapidly and so provide enough runs for their team to force victory in the time available, these surfaces brought their own difficulties. Larkins, Capel and Lamb, for example, were stroke-makers at Northampton whose talent would generally see them through but who would be periodically left vulnerable by a pitch's slowness. Hitting through the line of the ball with confidence in these conditions is not easy, and Lamb or Capel might play too soon and be caught in the infield. Larkins was sometimes exposed by a characteristically tight English seamer such as Yorkshire's Chris Old as he aimed firm-footed drives from the crease at a ball which failed to bounce or come on to the bat, with the result he was too often caught at slip or trapped lbw.

One answer to the twin problems of slow surfaces – bowlers failing to take wickets regularly enough and batsmen failing to find runs quickly enough – was to leave sufficient grass on the pitch both to bind the soil and to give the ball purchase for pace and lift. It was, of course, a solution which ultimately generated great dispute because medium-paced seamers were alleged to achieve excessive lateral movement off the pitch and thereby gain a level of success out of proportion to their ability.

At Trent Bridge the grassy pitches of the 1980s and their consequent degree of bounce made for several Nottinghamshire players with fine back-foot techniques. Batsmen like Chris Broad, Tim Robinson, Paul Johnson and Derek Randall all learned to cope with the lift and score runs with cuts, pulls and back-foot drives. Typically, a Northamptonshire batting line-up would go to Trent Bridge and lose the game because they were

81

unable to adapt their own more cramped methods. Similarly, Nottinghamshire would go to Northampton and be unable to force victory despite a superiority on paper. They would not be bowled out cheaply because their batting techniques, developed on faster pitches, were good enough to permit late adjustment, but they would find it difficult to score quickly enough to establish positions from which to direct the game's progress.

The confusion in the debate about pitches as they relate to the County Championship derives from a failure to establish precisely what purpose domestic first-class cricket is supposed to serve. Are we concerned to develop the best individual talents for higher representative honours, or should county cricket remain valid in itself, a source of good, tight play which can give satisfaction to the members and spectators who pay to watch it? It is no doubt true that the 'better' the surface upon which the game is played – that is, one that offers generous degrees of both natural pace and consistent lift – the better the cricketer who learns his trade in that environment, either as batsman or bowler. For the most part, pitches at the Oval enable batsmen to explore their skills naturally, without doubt or fear over inhibitory vagaries of pace or bounce. Under the same conditions, bowlers have to learn how to manipulate the ball and make the basic assets of line and length almost second nature.

A good Surrey batsman schooled at the Oval will essentially adjust down when he comes to Northampton, for example; the basics will serve him well, in that it will be difficult to get him out, but he will not be able to score his runs so quickly. Pacy, true pitches create batsmen who learn to play correctly both back and forward, and they oblige bowlers to maximise their ability in that those who do not habitually put the ball in the right place are badly exposed. Although it can legitimately be argued that these conditions do not always make for the best matches, in that runs come more readily than wickets, at least such pitches offer speed of scoring and the assurance that edges will carry to close catchers. What is absolute anathema to Championship cricket is the kind of pitch which, for fear of being pronounced too helpful to medium-pacers, combines the worst of all worlds.

This is the pitch which is not only weighted heavily in favour of the batsmen, but is also without pace or bounce because grass has been excluded. The lack of pace on otherwise true surfaces, the norm at Taunton in 1990 to give a notorious example, creates pudding-like pitches which do not in fact teach how to bat; they teach instead how to make 100s in circumstances where, if you are prepared to eliminate most risk, you will not be dismissed. Even with the best of cricketing wills, it is difficult to see how such pitches can take three-day games to a positive outcome without resort to those final afternoon declarations which make the preceding two and a half days largely meaningless.

The Championship points structure, however, places its entire emphasis on results, and so, in the late 1970s, certain good sides began to enjoy a significant in-built advantage. Those counties which undertook much of their cricket on little-used club grounds away from the county headquarters (Essex, Hampshire and Kent best illustrate the argument) could find squares which still retain enough unstifled life and character to produce both excellent matches and uncontrived results. It is hardly surprising, or even culpable surely, that other counties (Nottinghamshire being the 'offender' most usually cited) should have sought to redress this balance by the underpreparation of their pitches.

What, then, constitutes the best kind of Championship match, not in terms of the supposed benefits it will confer on future England Test players, but for the sustained tension and fascination it will offer to participant and spectator alike? It has first to be conceded that there is a finite limit to the number of runs a game can produce. Since three-day cricket, after the loss of time for changes between innings, involves a minimum of 313 overs when play is uninterrupted, it is almost certain to yield between 850 and 1150 runs, depending on the rate of scoring permitted by the pitch. If it is accepted that there is something intrinsically more fulfilling in a game where the time available can, as nearly as possible, be filled exactly by the natural course of four completed innings, it can be seen that, the moment any side exceeds even 300 runs, it is difficult for this 'ideal' scenario to come about.

In practice, a spectator will invariably be assured a fine game if each side's score on first innings is around the 250 mark. For such totals to be reached, there will almost certainly be a keen and close contest. Someone will show that runs can be scored by the batsman who plays well and, equally, if the bowlers perform to their fullest – or batsmen fail to concentrate – wickets will fall. Keith Fletcher would always say that the perfect first-innings score was 260; from such a beginning you would know that you had a game of cricket before you. If the side batting second fights hard enough – or is bowled at sufficiently poorly – it will get ahead and seek to bowl out the opposition cheaply a second time. Alternatively, if 260 has represented the optimum use of a pitch at its best, it should now yield progressively less runs and provide a conclusion exactly inside the game's distance.

The reply to a first innings which has realised only 250 or so will often be the most important part of the tight game. The side which has batted may now bowl badly either because it is unconsciously waiting for the pitch to do the job or, more familiarly, because it carries into the field a sense of resentment at its earlier batting inadequacy. Alternatively, the side batting second may be so intimidated by fears both of the pitch and of a low-scoring reply that its batting is inhibited by an attitude which lacks the requisite fight or gumption.

Relatively low-scoring matches bring out great differences in field placement. On a pitch which looks as if it will induce a regular fall of wickets, one type of captain will immediately have three slips, a gully and a forward short-leg . Another will argue, 'Yes, we can get people out', but place such a premium on preventing unnecessary runs that he allows himself only three close catchers. It is dangerously easy for captains to adopt the Test-match mentality of aggressive fields without anticipating early enough the possible development of the game as a whole. Kim Barnett of Derbyshire, if sometimes guilty of being rather negative and safety-first in his declarations, is in these situations a very underrated captain. Despite an armoury of seam bowlers, he still analyses both the opposition and the pitch with great care and is most adept at taking wickets by applying pressure through fielding positions which are not overtly attacking. Even if a pitch offers a degree of movement, he will carefully assess its pace and therefore the probabilities of exactly where the ball will go.

The biggest decision will often come down to whether or not to place a third slip, a gully or a third man for a particular batsman. Such options need to be assessed very quickly indeed by both the captain and his bowlers in the context of the game's likely overall direction, as half an hour of indecisive experimentation in tight games can surrender all. Ten overs of attack which fail to come off can result in the concession of precisely those runs which, in the final analysis, win the match. Even when the ball was swinging, Essex's John Lever, if he believed the match might ultimately be won and lost by the odd boundary, would place a man at deep backward square-leg for Wayne Larkins. He believed that it was more important to check Larkins's ability to flick an in-swinger off his pads for 4 than to retain the limited chance of a catch at third slip.

It is evident from this example that one of the reasons why the closest Championship fixtures are so interesting to watch and to play in is that they draw so critically on facets of the professional game which are not always apparent when ability alone brings overwhelming supremacy. When a dedicated bowler such as Lever achieves success by exercising his cricketing intelligence, the response of his opponents, who mix admiration and respect with embarrassment and even bitterness that they have been outwitted, is very revealing. On a wider plane, teams will betray a certain humiliated shock when they realise that the opposition has recognised something that they themselves have failed to see because they have been unable to look beyond the stereotypical norm. An example here might be when the side batting on into the second day incurs the undisguised resentment of the opposition, because they have read signs of deterioration in a pitch which their opponents have missed, and have thus secured the advantage.

Less graphically, tight games can slip away in the course of an hour because the fielding side's effort, application or concentration has lapsed even minimally. Alternatively, from a batting perspective, wickets may be surrendered precisely because the fielding side is allowed to grasp the initiative. Under the pressure of the crucial moment, indeterminate play and a lack of resolve discloses itself to the fielders, enhancing their sense of ascendancy and spurring them to perform even more keenly. The best teams are, to a man, alive to those minutes when the game's outcome will be decided, and it is exactly at such times that each player, in the argot of the circuit, 'raises his game'. For the batsman, a good 60 or 70 in the tightest of matches will mean much more than many a comfortable century; for the bowler, the slightest relaxation of pressure or loss of nerve during a vital ten overs can cost the game. For this reason low-scoring games are often won by the side with the right attitude at the right moment rather than by the side with the greater ability on paper.

Teams are sometimes said to 'know how to win'. Beneath the mystique this means, in practice, that they maintain unremitting standards of concentration and that each man assesses the developing pattern of the game for himself. It is almost as if everyone is intuitively detecting the next turning point in the game's narrative without need of instruction or encouragement from above: each team member is thinking like a captain.

The best Championship cricket, then, usually results from pitches which, by a happy combination of perhaps unrelated factors, provide reasonable encouragement for both bat and ball. Given the variety of squares around the country, each with its own problems for the groundsman, these are not the pitches which the TCCB's guidelines for 1990 would ordinarily produce. But priorities have become confused, and if the TCCB's intention is to create even contests which will bring about natural conclusions in the last session of a game, then the only valid directive to groundsmen is to aim for that very goal. Moreover, the player forged by such competitive cricket is precisely the one better able to cope, surely, with the demands at Test level. The argument has been that Championship pitches need to be 'excellent' to foster Test-calibre skills. In the 1990–91 Ashes series, however, the difference between the two sides lay not so much in skill, but in ability under pressure. Again and again England collapsed at critical moments or failed to press home a decisive advantage in the field.

Undeniably, the ideal pitch is far more easily defined than created. But it would require clubs not to look at things too selfishly or narrowly in terms of producing guaranteed, two-day 'result' pitches, but to address the real question of how to coax

1. A traditional unchanging rite of summer? Mark Robinson, Nigel Felton and Alan Fordham receive their Northamptonshire caps from Allan Lamb. Much is in fact concealed here: Robinson left for Yorkshire a month later, Felton had spent seven earlier seasons at Somerset, and Fordham, after university studies, was already 25.

2. Players may spend most dressing-room time talking about horses, sponsored cars, music and women but their discourse off the field can be unexpectedly serious. Here Nigel Felton, Nick Cook, Geoff Cook and David Capel keep their thoughts to themselves, although both Cooks have found the racing page.

3 & 4. *(left)* Commitment is one undoubted requirement for success. Watched by umpire Kevin Lyons, his own concentration quite evident, Richard Williams employs his spinning finger. *(right)* Commitment is not unambiguous, however. On the field Peter Willey gives everything; off it he looks after himself almost obsessively. There is just a hint to this ethic of something approaching tragedy.

5 & 6. *(left)* 'If only we had eleven Alan Walkers, we'd be a much better team'. But is absolute commitment a real substitute for match-winning talent? *(right)* David Steele prepares for a new season in 1978. There is a new stress today on set regimes and the cultivation of corporate identity, even in approaches to training.

7. Although Nick Cook's studied clowning tries to suggest otherwise, he is a deeply sensitive man whose passionate engagement of cricket forever betrays itself to the camera. Umpire Bird, perhaps fearful of an appeal, is obliged to retreat.

8. The best teams are – to a man – alive to those moments when the game's outcome will be decided. Alan Walker communicates his concern to his captain and suggests a change of approach.

9 & 10. *(above)* Whatever else success entails, it obviously demands ability. The contemporary opener who is not adept at back-foot play will have a very brief life-span. Wayne Larkins negotiates a rising ball as Deryck Murray, Clive Lloyd and Viv Richards anticipate frailty. *(below)* In complete contrast, Rob Bailey goes massively forward. Bailey has been criticised for his front-foot method, yet he grew up on very slow surfaces which were turgid and lacking in bounce.

11 & 12. *(left)* Talent takes many forms, as Tim Lamb perhaps demonstrates. *(right)* An altogether more classical study of high-calibre swing bowling. Pakistan have produced a sequence of bowlers with genuine specialist skills, and no Championship opponent was more formidable in the 1970s than Sarfraz Nawaz.

13. Lancashire experience the peaks of elation in the one-day game at Northamptonshire's expense, as Larkins becomes the third of Phil DeFreitas's victims in an opening spell of 8–4–19–5 which effectively won the 1990 NatWest Trophy Final in the first hour. Hegg, Atherton, Allott, Fairbrother and Hughes salute his triumph.

14. Crowds, and in truth little else, validate the one-day game. The queues lengthen along the terraced streets of Northampton before the 1990 NatWest Trophy quarter-final.

15. The emotions aroused by one-day triumph or defeat are extreme if transitory. Northampton-shire beat Essex to win the 1980 Benson and Hedges Cup: left to right, Geoff Cook, Sarfraz (obscured), Allan Lamb, Jim Watts, Tim Lamb (obscured), George Sharp, Richard Williams . . .

16. . . . but lose to Yorkshire in the 1987 Benson and Hedges Cup Final. Allan Lamb, Richard Williams, Duncan Wild and Rob Bailey offer further expressions which speak for themselves.

17 & 18. *(above)* County cricket proceeds on a day-to-day basis, evoking at various stages the whole range of human emotion. On 11 July 1987 Yorkshire won the Benson and Hedges Cup Final by losing fewer wickets in a tied match. David Ripley is left numbed, Roger Harper grim-faced. *(below)* For his part, an ashen, drawn and exhausted David Capel turns away from the throng. His innings had been perhaps the best in the match, his bowling analysis the weakest.

19. In 1989 Dennis Lillee returned to Northampton for a month in a specifically coaching capacity, but was ready to offer his help to any player on the circuit who sought it. Here the touring Australian Merv Hughes gains the benefit, though evidently not of his advice.

20 & 21. *(left)* At Chelmsford, on 17 September 1988, Lillee began the last afternoon of his professional career by winning a bet with Allan Lamb. Graham Gooch allowed this ball to pass, the umpire made no signal and six more deliveries were then bowled. A seven-ball over: one by the Ancient Mariner, six by the ancient Dennis. *(right)* Roger Harper, another marvellous thinker on the game who was always prepared to discuss its principles, is found in rather more lyrical mood.

good, open cricket from squares which are tired and mori-
bund. This is not an issue resolved by blanket instructions to
groundsmen on 'correct' preparation: individual circumstances
almost certainly require individual solutions. The need is for
administrators to agree on the purpose of Championship cricket
and then to trust to the groundsman's local knowledge and
experience even where, for example, this involves the use of
grass to revive otherwise plasticine pitches.

The other main pitch-related problem which has rightly
roused such concern over the last ten years is the near-extinction
of the spinner, who would also benefit greatly from any redis-
covery of bounce at county grounds. But matters are inherently
more difficult for the spinner in that his revival relies more
heavily on the compliance of the weather. In an ideal summer,
with sunshine through July and August, the spinner will have his
day on dry and dusting squares just as the seamer thrived in the
early-season damp and the swing bowler prospered whenever
atmospheric conditions allowed. The elements, alas, are rarely
so obliging. There is certainly an argument for the uncovering
of pitches with the specific aim of helping slow bowlers – that is,
the run-ups must be exposed, too – but there is little chance that
commercial interests will consent to this. If the pitch is exposed
at all times within a match, starts are inevitably delayed; if
only uncovered during play, the pressure falls on the umpires
to suspend proceedings early to ensure a prompt resumption
next day. These were the problems encountered in 1987 when
a limited uncovering experiment was last attempted.

A more realistic hope for the spinner's return might be in
a full Championship programme of four-day matches; unless
pitches are altered to permit finishes without contrivance, such
a programme would probably in itself be beneficial. There is
a degree to which players must accept their own responsibility
for the problem of artificial Championship cricket. In their
insistence upon 110 overs a day as the maximum they will
accept, they help to establish a pattern of play to which regular
supporters must all too often resign themselves. Side A wins
the toss and declares shortly before the close of the first day at
around 350. Side B declares 50 behind after tea on the second
day, enabling Side A to gain a lead of 150 by the close. They then

offer a run chase after lunch on the third day of approximately 280 in 60 overs. This sounds rather cynical; in the last ten years or so, however, it has been all too common.

One element in the 1990 rethinking of pitch guidelines, the introduction of penalties for sub-standard surfaces, and the reduction of the number of strands in the seam of the ball, was the desire to revitalise swing bowling by nullifying the journeyman seamer. The real point about the mediocre medium-pacer on a poor pitch was not that he could take wickets, but that his bad deliveries escaped punishment; on slow pitches batsmen could rarely commit themselves to the attacking shot for fear that the ball would not 'come on'. The desire to encourage swing bowling is entirely laudable; its potency cannot be overemphasised, and when a top-quality swing bowler comes into the game (as Imran Khan did in the early 1970s, for example, and Terry Alderman in the early 1980s) his effect is such that, for a while, batsmen prove almost incapable of playing him. In late May 1990 Surrey brought off a coup by signing the young Pakistani, Waqar Younis, and immediately his fast, full, late swing (out towards the slips but mainly in to the batsman's leg stump) was quite devastating, even on Oval pitches where batsmen had been so dominant.

The challenge of confronting high-calibre swing bowling is for many batsmen the high point of their careers, as the contest places such a supreme onus on technique. It is essential that the bat is straight, that the amount of swing is judged early and that the out-swinger can be distinguished immediately from the in-swinger. The head and body must be kept perfectly still, so that the batsman can give himself a fixed standpoint against which to assess accurately how the ball is moving. As a generalisation, the back-foot method will be more vulnerable, a theory which has sometimes guided England's selection of bowlers against the West Indies, certainly at home. The essence of the confrontation, however, is that it is intensely individual and solitary. Some batsmen attempt to read the swing through the air, others watch carefully to see which side of the ball the bowler is holding, others again pick up slight differences in action which can alert them to the bowler's intentions. Arthur Milton, the veteran Gloucestershire and England opener, would always adjust his guard to off stump against real out-swing on the basis that anything which moved away from his body could then be safely left; a prime part of the art of playing swing is ensuring that the bat is employed as little as possible.

The problem with such bowling, however, is that it is such a personal attribute that not only has it never been fully explained, it can also desert a bowler almost as quickly as it was found. In broad outline, the best swing bowling will demand a perfect side-on action, a high arm and the positive propulsion of the ball from the hand with a wrist action rather than simply letting it go. Formidable swing, of a kind which can dominate Championship seasons or win Test series, will involve late movement from a full length rather than long, superficially impressive curves from the hand. Yet swing of this quality is a matter of fine, if not minute, margins. Unconscious alterations to a bowler's rhythm and technique suddenly deprive him of what was hitherto virtually guaranteed success. The Australian Bob Massie came to prominence overnight for his match-winning analyses in the Lord's Test of 1972 and was forgotten almost as instantly, his action imperceptibly upset by subsequent injury. Kent's Richard Ellison effectively won the Ashes series of 1985 with controlled swing in the final two Tests, but, cruelly, this had all but vanished by the following summer.

There is also an extent to which batsmen come to grips with previously inscrutable bowlers by beginning to absorb the experience of facing them. The process is largely unconscious, but certain consistent elements in the bowler's approach or action become associated with predictable effects and some of the alarm is thereby removed. It would be true to say that no great bowler in recent times has maintained his status by swing bowling alone.

Alderman, after the full power of his out-swing had deserted him through injury, compensated by becoming metronomically accurate. Both Richard Hadlee and Dennis Lillee had far more to their armouries than the modest swing they could always employ for variety. Their secret was that they had so conquered line and length that they had absolute confidence in their ability not to bowl bad balls. From this secure base they were then able to experiment with subtle adjustments of wrist action, masterly changes in pace and length or variations to the delivery stride. Hadlee's classic definition likens an over to a gun: it contains six separate shots, of which not all are intended to hit, but each has a conscious, preparatory relationship to the one which completes the kill.

We have referred to the 1990 season as one of considerable change in the emphasis of the Championship. It was then that the TCCB's pitches consultant, Harry Brind, demonstrated to his colleagues the 'authorised' Championship surface – one without moisture, which was either white or straw-coloured, certainly devoid of grass, and which offered consistent bounce (or, in the event, lack of bounce). At the same time the TCCB reduced the number of strands in the seam of the ball.

The theory, or at least the hope, which prompted the widespread change in pitch preparation was that dormant bowling skills would be rediscovered, and the experiment seems set to continue for some time to come. But the 'bowling skills' to be rekindled were, in effect if not in conscious design, the skills of the faster bowlers; that pitches remained covered offered no encouragement to spinners. If slow bowlers took a greater proportion of wickets in 1990 they did so, in the main, because they bowled more. It is wishful thinking to seek a return to lost arts in the sheer number of overs delivered by spinners, but far more typical was the introduction of the spinners for two-hour spells as a sign of despair on the part of the captain that his seamers would ever achieve a breakthrough. The lot of the slow bowler was thus to fill the breach while his faster colleagues were withdrawn from further, unnecessary punishment. Of the regular Championship venues perhaps only two, Old Trafford and New Road, Worcester, consistently offered the spinners slow turn in 1990, and even traditional spinners' pitches such as Bournemouth, Cheltenham and Folkestone failed to deviate from the bat-dominated norm.

One of the very few games to provide considerable assistance to the slow bowler from an early stage was between Kent and Leicestershire at Dartford, and that was immediately subject to TCCB scrutiny and the threat of a points deduction hung over the pitch for some days. Yet the average innings total there was 230 and, while admittedly only two other batsmen managed scores in excess of 40, Kent's Mark Benson illustrated what an excellent left-hand technique could achieve in making 107. Sadly, it was no surprise to find Hesketh Park deprived of its one first-class fixture for 1991 for fear that it would again incur unfavourable comment. This was not a sensitivity induced by 1990 alone, but it has been an all too familiar response to pitches which, in recent seasons, have offered any marked help to spinners.

What were the actual results of the changes to Championship cricket in 1990? The records for the number both of centuries and double centuries in a first-class season were broken, and individual batting averages were universally inflated to the extent of some 10 runs per innings. If this arguably reversed the previous trend for medium-pace bowlers to gain wickets too cheaply, the effect on the type of play a spectator could anticipate in Championship games was to produce a state of drear predictability. It is worth repeating that the ideal game involves an average all-out score of around 250. In a four-day game this can be increased to 325 or so, but the TCCB remains committed to three times as many three-day as four-day matches. If the concern is to create Championship cricket which is worthwhile in itself, as opposed to nurturing alleged Test skills, the length of available playing time must surely be the prime influence on the kinds of pitches which are prepared.

Despite the 'result' wickets which prevailed then, 40 per cent of those games in the 1980s which had a positive result rather than the draw did so on the basis of a final-day declaration. In 1990 this increased to 52 per cent. It is important to enunciate here, then, that 1990 simply made more pronounced a trend which has long held sway in the proving ground of English cricket. Yet so pronounced was the supremacy of the bat that summer that almost exactly half of these 'declaration games' were won by the side which chased a target, rather than the one which set it. In other words, all that had preceded the final afternoon, in seven sessions of usually high run-scoring, was largely meaningless: half the results were decided in conditions akin to those of the second innings of an extended one-day match. The only differences are, first, that in order to win one side has to bowl the other out and, second, that the team chasing the runs does not automatically lose if the target is not met. Nevertheless, 1990 placed even greater emphasis on the ability, on the one hand, to score quick last-innings runs and, on the other, to bowl containingly against a post-tea thrash. These are hardly the skills most appropriate to Test matches.

While the best sides unquestionably achieved their prominence by the traditional and legitimate means of dismissing an opponent twice (Worcestershire, for example, achieved five of their seven victories in 1990 by offering a target and then taking 10 wickets), other counties profited inordinately from run chases. Warwickshire finished in the top five by gaining three out of their seven wins in successful pursuit of last-innings runs; for Glamorgan it was three out of five, Yorkshire four out of five, and Sussex two out of three. The targets in these run chases also reflected the greater imbalance towards the bat. The ability of Hampshire to attain 445 to win on the last day of the season would be exceptional in any year, but the standard declaration began to invite 340 or so at a rate of 5 per over rather than the 280 in 60 overs which we proposed was the 1980s norm. Three-day games which result in either of these targets being set have overreached the time available to them. Captains have confessed to going out to toss knowing in advance, from the likely state of the pitch, that there lay ahead of them precisely such final-day scenarios which, in effect, consigned the first two days to formal manoeuvring. For whose benefit, then, and to what end, are the bulk of such matches played?

The reply has been, of course, that they are for the benefit of the England Test side. Yet the logic of this argument is compromised by the TCCB's continuing refusal both to cut back the amount of one-day cricket played in a season and to move further towards a programme of four-day games. There is palpable inconsistency here. If the proposition is that bowling attacks should return to an environment which demands the kind of skills outlined above, then the one-day calendar must also be amended. For this, far more than green Championship pitches, has been the central cause of decline, and it is difficult to conceive of even one positive gain that bowlers have made from playing limited-overs cricket, most especially from playing in the

Sunday League. One-day games appear sacrosanct, however, and the Championship alone, to the detriment of its interest as a source of gripping play, has been the site of experimentation.

Looking again at 1990, which bowlers may we say exhibited levels of skill which had hitherto been absent? Or, more appropriately, who confirmed the potential which had previously lacked a regular incentive for development? There were arguably only four seamers who made the kind of progress the change was designed to stimulate: Surrey's Martin Bicknell, Leicestershire's Chris Lewis, Warwickshire's Tim Munton and Nottinghamshire's Andy Pick. None of these bowlers was particularly a revelation: each was known to have certain abilities, although it may well be that these abilities were brought more consistently to the fore by the general absence of pitches which seamed lavishly. At the same time, however, at least five times their number were set back. It was not a case of these bowlers being 'found out' by the relative ease of batting conditions, but of their being badly demoralised by the denial of reasonable support for their own specific, and not inconsiderable, degrees of skill. Men like Derbyshire's Simon Base, Essex's Don Topley and Hampshire's P. J. Bakker, or even recent Test caps such as Phil DeFreitas and Kent's Alan Igglesden, too often found themselves the foil for displays of run-gathering, frequently by batsmen whose own limitations were in fact far more severe than those of the bowlers.

But this, it will be said, is precisely what was desired: a few made the right advances, the majority were exposed. Passing seasons will eventually make the majority adapt also, and the changes will be vindicated. It may well be that, by the time these words are read, two or three more bowlers will have been unearthed who have honed new talents. The process is not, however, open-ended. Even if a decade of batting dominance were eventually to produce a general rise in bowling standards, it would represent ten years of far from satisfying domestic cricket.

The evidence from other countries and earlier eras is not very heartening. Domestic cricket in India and Pakistan has for years been played on dead pitches weighted in favour of the batsmen. Yet innings scores in those countries remain for the most part high, and the balance has not been redressed by a wide spread of advanced bowling skills. At Test level, plasticine pitches on the sub-continent have often encouraged extreme pace, great swing bowling and a range of superb, specialist spin, but the cricketers in question have represented the pinnacles of their art, men who would arguably be led by Test-match conditions to develop their excellence anyway. In the 1930s in England Championship pitches, at least where rain had not affected them, made for a similar supremacy of bat over ball. Again, certain Test-winning attributes, from the pace of Harold Larwood, Bill Voce and Bill Bowes to the spin of Hedley Verity, were perhaps nurtured in certain cricketers who remained both far superior to their peers and very limited in number. A general levelling of the contest between ball and bat did not occur: the decade ended as it had begun, with batsmen decidedly on top.

Absent from the debate on Championship cricket has been an element which might rationally be thought most crucial: what makes matches attractive for the hardy spectators who pay to watch them? The question has been at least obliquely acknowledged by the re-emergence at the highest level of an old thesis: crowds love to see runs being scored. This may once have been true of the thousands who flocked to watch domestic cricket in the 1930s, but it is not true of the contemporary member. Members today, watching the Championship daily in little more than hundreds, are far less passive in their relationship to the entertainment before them and, as a minority consciously pursuing cricket above other interests, they usually understand the implications of what they see. They can differentiate between centuries which point to a 'declaration match' and centuries which may win uncontrived games. The one continuing attraction is success; witness the crowds who have watched Essex and Worcestershire in recent seasons. But the attitude amongst regulars in 1990 was often that they were being vaguely cheated. As yet another score of 390–6 declared ensured that all would again rest on the last afternoon, discerning members found less and less to engage their cricketing intelligence.

At the crux of this is the issue of the 'perfect match'. If your allegiances lie with the Championship *aficionado*, then games should ideally reach 'natural' conclusions; too often, however, he or she is the last person to be considered. And surely such 'real' cricket, where the effort expended has a demonstrable bearing on results, is itself the best preparation for Tests. The prevailing line of reason has been that if bowlers need only to hit the seam to gain success they will explore their art no further. The other side of the coin, however, and one very evident in contemporary Championship play, is that, since a bowler's full range of improvisation still cannot prevent sides scoring 375 runs, attack becomes a waste of energy. The rational, less arduous option is to develop defensive skills, the precise opposite of what was sought.

In the last analysis, the appropriate balance between bat and ball should hardly be a mystery, but will follow from the length of time set aside for a match. An all-out score of 150, for example, is not an absolute offence: it was by no means uncommon in 19th-century cricket and would be a near-necessity if Championship games lasted only two days. Since the Championship match is, for three-quarters of the season, of three days, and Tests last for five, 150 – given that a side has batted to its fullest capacity – would suggest an unacceptable pitch. Few would disagree with this. But, in the interests of an uncontrived finish, the score of 375, where attained comfortably, is equally unacceptable. This has been altogether less readily conceded.

Such thinking enables us to ask the question, 'When is the pitch to be labelled "poor"?' Before all else, perhaps, the element of physical danger is paramount. If a pitch is two-paced then it may rightly be criticised by batsmen. Balls which, although pitching on approximately the same spot, are as likely to scuttle through low as they are to rear towards a batsman's chin clearly present an unacceptable physical threat. When he plays right forward to a good-length delivery to counter movement off the seam or the chance of low bounce, a batsmen has the right to expect that it will not suddenly spit from the pitch and break a finger on his bottom hand.

This much would be universally accepted in the professional game. Batting demands courage, but it must be a courage founded on the reasonable expectation that a bowler's varied methods can be at least theoretically countered. If the bowler bowls short or with a change of pace, the bounce can be anticipated, the batsman's wrists slackened and his movement on to the front foot checked. If the batsman is still struck on the body, he can accept his error. It is when a ball behaves in a way that nobody could really have predicted that he is entitled to blame the pitch.

Surfaces like this have always been very rare in the Championship. The most notorious recent example of such vagary of bounce was seen in 1989 at Trent Bridge. Shortly after the start of the second day in Nottinghamshire's match with Derbyshire, a game in which 21 wickets had already fallen in seven hours and several batsmen had been hit, umpires Barry Meyer and Peter Wight ordered that play should be halted and resumed on a different pitch. The decision, influenced by the presence in the match of men of the speed of Franklyn Stephenson and Michael Holding, was almost certainly unique in the history of English first-class cricket.

Other assessments of unacceptability are much less straight-forward. We can argue that a pitch is inadequate if sides which have batted well and applied themselves totally are unable to score sufficient runs at an acceptable rate to carry the game well into a third day – towards tea, perhaps. The reference to tempo here is important. It is quite conceivable that a pitch can be so devoid of pace that, although overall scores are well below average, the match will still not be completed. Batsmen may not be able to score fluent runs but they are able to survive at length by patient, self-denying graft.

In 1988 Northamptonshire played Hampshire at Bourne-mouth and, in an uninterrupted match, the first three innings totals were 239, 205 and 164–9 declared. These runs had come at an average of 2.29 per over. For that reason, it seemed cautious of Mark Nicholas to set Northamptonshire 199 for victory at a rate of 4.33. As it proved, Northamptonshire were immediately in trouble at 46–4 but were able to bat out time to reach 108–7 at the close and gain the draw. Although the mean total in the match was 194, a fact which would ordinarily have indicated a finish well inside eight sessions, it was ultimately unsatisfying for the spectators. In periods they were offered compelling, attritional cricket but overall they lacked even a gripping climax to compensate for the absence of attractive runs. More to the point, it became apparent by the second day that a draw was the likeliest outcome. Nevertheless, Northamptonshire might well have won that match if they had held their catches, and a side like Essex or Middlesex could possibly have forced victory despite the slowness of the pitch.

It is a persistent, if forgivable, failing of batsmen that they should blame the conditions for their own lack of application. Outside the positively dangerous circumstances outlined above, it is doubtful whether there really is such a thing in cricket as the 'unplayable' ball. West Indian all-rounder Roger Harper, a marvellous thinker on the game who was always prepared to discuss its principles, argued that it was possible to imagine a ball which swung very late into the batsman, pitched on leg and then flew away past the off stump. Quite apart from the fact that this probably would not dismiss the batsman anyway, the rest of his dressing-room colleagues would dispute that such a delivery was physically feasible.

Incidentally, any judgement based on the first innings alone is unfair both to the pitch and to the groundsman who prepared it. There are many county venues where the pitch flattens out and eases as the match continues, the bounce becoming lower and slower. Far from deteriorating to give hope of a close finish, such squares must be given a degree of early life for there to be any realistic chance of a natural conclusion.

Although the fascination of Championship cricket is that its possible permutations are almost limitless, a few rough generalisations may be welcome. For example, much depends on precisely how low the first-innings scores are. If they are both around 240–260, the potential is for the most rewarding and continuously enthralling of Championship fixtures. Ideally, this will be a fluctuating match which, without need of declarations, comes to the tightest of conclusions in the last 20 overs. It is never quite possible to say with any assurance in these games which side is on top; from hour to hour the balance of forces seems to be in the ratio 55:45, first in favour of one side, then in favour of the other.

If the totals are around 185 or less the match may well be just as gripping, but the chance for individual talents and attitudes to dictate the outcome will probably be diminished. The match may perhaps end well inside the distance. Yet the most typical pattern in the Championship is where both sides reach 300, and with it full batting points, within the 100 overs available to them. If good rates of progress can be maintained (3.5 runs or more per over) then the side replying will probably declare after tea on the second day and concede a first-innings lead. One of the keys to the last day is then the size of the overnight lead which can be carried forward by the side batting first as it begins its second innings.

Overnight leads of around 150 to 200 will offer the chance of third-afternoon declarations that can set extended run chases over some 60 to 70 overs. The ideal situation at the close of the second day is perhaps for the side batting first to be not only 150 or so ahead, but 4 or 5 wickets down. This makes it more likely that their declaration will be pre-empted by dismissal: the run chase is accordingly more inclined to be a realistic one and, perversely, will probably give both sides a better chance of victory.

If a side's reply to a low score gives it a considerable lead, then the captain must decide exactly how long he wants to bat, whether to commit the opposition to the prospect of fighting only for the draw, and what length of time his attack will need to dismiss them a second time. If the side batting first gains a big first-innings lead, however, they will need to score as quickly as possible at the second attempt to leave the maximum number of overs to bowl the opposition out again. These games can be the most frustrating for sides if they have dominated seven sessions only to be defeated when the opposition unexpectedly achieve the target set for them.

Championship cricket is not in reality anything like as simple as these patterns may suggest. The variations on each theme are legion, and are complicated by changes in conditions and circumstances which can wholly upset a team's strategy. This has always been one of the game's principal and definitive features. For example, a side coming out to bat again after tea on the second day, with a lead of 125 on first innings, suddenly finds that the skies have clouded over and the opposition attack, annoyed with itself for its first-innings failure, is determined to recover lost ground. Caught between an initial desire to pursue further rapid runs and the fear that wickets are falling too regularly, the team makes its indecisive way to 100–7 at the close. The opponents, reinvigorated by the momentum of their fight-back, can now anticipate the prospect of making 260 or so at a rate of 3 per over to win on the last day.

Although it is true that most batsmen will derive greater satisfaction from 50s scored in adversity than from centuries at their ease, matches where runs come readily remain very much examinations of attitude. The mental approach dictated by difficult circumstances, where a batsman's life expectancy will be short, is one which seeks to employ technique merely for survival. It is easier to play with freedom on a good pitch, where the batsman allows his arms to go through with the shot, confident that the ball will not deviate and that his timing will not be undermined by an unpredictable bounce. Shot selection becomes less problematic, and the player achieves what is invariably described as 'fluency'.

Professional batsmen are irritated by what they believe to be ill-informed comments on their style, and nothing annoys them more than criticism which takes no account of the conditions in which they are operating. This might suggest that they have lost touch or that they are not 'in the mood' when an innings of dazzling stroke-play is followed in the next match by one of circumspection. The insult will be compounded when, after falling to a lapse of concentration, they are accused of having played a 'loose' or 'stupid' shot. Such exasperation with unfair censure is caused by the player's acute sensitivity to the fact that batting is never 'good' in itself, but is only appropriate or inappropriate to the demands of a team in specific conditions and circumstances.

It is therefore common on good Championship surfaces for the batsman to apply himself too jealously to the preservation of his wicket. The lure of the big innings beckons, but runs fail to come quickly enough for the needs of both the side and the game. In effect, the fear of losing his wicket on a pitch which should assure a statistically impressive performance distorts his reading of the game. All batsmen must be permitted to play themselves in regardless of the quality of the strip; what is harmful to his team is evident only after that, when acceleration fails to arrive.

If, on a good wicket, the side batting first reaches 300 in 85 overs with several wickets in hand, it can increase the tempo yet further and seek 400–410 by the close of the first day's play. This commits the opposition to scoring rather more runs in reply on the second day if they are to achieve a balance acceptable to them by the start of the third day. Unless this is dictated by the certainty that the pitch will deteriorate rapidly, however, the plan places even greater emphasis on the need for swift progress: if the side batting first has batted to lunch on the second day for its major score, insufficient time will remain to bowl the opposition out twice.

The foresight required of cricketers, then, is considerable. Although most batsmen will realise the need to pace their innings in a run chase, far fewer bring an equally alert approach to their batting at the first attempt. A good side does not bat recklessly or with unnecessary flamboyance in the first innings but it does seek every opportunity to advance positively even on the opening morning, in the understanding that a substantial total of enterprising runs increases the routes to victory available to the captain.

Sunil Gavaskar best fulfilled the need for something beyond mere technical ability. He was the model of the complete opening batsman, as shown by his record of thirteen centuries against the West Indies, an achievement all the more astounding for a man who was brought up on dead Indian pitches with little experience of fast bowling. Although Gavaskar undoubtedly possessed a full array of perfectly executed shots, it was his ability to assess the nature of a pitch and the imperatives of a game which was so striking. In short, his strokes were selected in accordance with the widest demands of a context.

England played the third one-day international of their 1981–82 Indian tour at Cuttack, an occasional Test venue which produced a highly dubious pitch. The feeling in the visitors' dressing-room was that their score of 230 in a 46-over game would be comfortably defended if each bowler could keep it tight. Gavaskar then came out to offer a quite brilliant innings of uniquely virtuoso stroke-play, scoring 71 at a run a ball to win the game for his country. Three weeks earlier on the last day of the fourth Test, with England needing a win to square the series, Gavaskar had batted for six hours in difficult conditions for a magnificently self-restrained 83 not out to save the match. To those who watched both innings it was hard to credit the strength of mind which could enable Gavaskar to adapt so totally. His ability to wed perception to execution was breathtaking.

It is probably not surprising that in relatively high-scoring games there is a drift sometimes towards stagnation. Rather than manipulate events, sides settle for run rates of 3 an over, 4 batting points apiece and mutual cancellation by five o'clock on the second afternoon. Captaincy in Championship cricket too readily opts for the tried and tested. When a team is replying to a first day score of 350, for example, there is nothing to prevent an early declaration which would sacrifice a batting bonus point, but it would at least ask the attack to bowl well at the second attempt or to induce poor play by containment. A captain who made such a declaration would accept the onus to create victory for himself rather then relying on run chases.

Once every couple of rounds of Championship fixtures, one particular match is seen to be going nowhere, and runs are given away for perhaps the hour before lunch on the third day to make a declaration possible. Two batsmen who do not even bowl in the nets are introduced to the attack to add anything up to 150 to a total in 20 overs. In reality, this compensates for no more than about 25 overs earlier in the game when its development was allowed to wander, and a lead is developed which could well have been realised by more productive batting or more imaginative declarations on the first two days.

There are circumstances in which this liberality is necessary – where weather interruptions have upset the best intentions of both sides, for example. In the main, however, such contrivance is a blight on the game, a matter of fraud. Known variously as 'joke' bowling or 'declaration' bowling, it is more aptly described by the players as 'filth'. Complaint usually centres on the meaningless record-breaking which these circumstances so often involve. This should hardly be the concern: in its complete disavowal of what makes cricket so distinctive a test of skill and intelligence, the practice condemns itself. If a defence is to be found for the conservatism which ultimately underlies 'joke' bowling, it is perhaps in the Championship bonus point system. There is a lack of logic in a structure which will give maximum points to sides who find themselves level with only

113 overs remaining in the match, which is exactly the result of two teams making 300 all out in their respective 100 overs.

Less clear-cut is the extent to which conservatism also underpins another Championship scenario, seen more often now with the introduction of four-day cricket but not unknown in the shorter game. If a side has been dismissed for 180 in 60 overs, a performance well under par for the pitch, the dominant professional instinct in their opponents will be to play them completely out of the game by scoring, say, 450 in 160 overs. The first side is then committed to batting through the remainder of the match simply to gain the draw: even at a run rate of 3 an over, they will only have drawn level by the close of the last day.

Yet if the side batting second could reply slightly more rapidly, to score, say, 370 at 3 an over and then declare, their opponents would have the chance to clear their first-innings deficit, but they themselves would leave more overs in which to bowl them out again. Should the side batting first reach even 315 at a rate of 3 an over, and with it a lead of 125, then 25 overs will remain for the side batting second to get these runs, having gained fifteen extra, potentially critical, bowling overs.

The arithmetic here is less relevant than the principle. Professional cricketers are decidedly disinclined to surrender voluntarily any of the advantage they have fought for. They are equally reluctant to risk disaster in the last innings by leaving themselves with runs to chase, even though they will happily pursue targets in four or five Championship matches each summer. There is in fact sound psychological reasoning behind this apparent illogic: a side which has absolutely nothing to play for other than the draw is much more likely to capitulate than a side which has the prospect, however improbable, of causing a last-minute upset.

In 1988, in only the second four-day fixture to be played at Northampton, Warwickshire made 415 and dismissed the home side for 170. Following on, Northamptonshire made 363 and then won the match by bowling out Warwickshire for 112, seven runs short of what had seemed certain victory. This wonderful game could hardly be thought typical: it was the first time Northamptonshire had won after following on in eighty-two years! It was probably enough, however, to make both sides think very carefully for a while before ever inviting a come-back, however slender its likelihood of success. In circumstances such as this, captaincy decisions depend not only on an assessment of the pitch, but on an understanding of the opposition's character. Some sides are prone to succumb in these situations, while others seem almost to relish the fighting draw more than a convincing victory.

As for the cricketers who tend more and more to be forgotten, maligned medium-pacers and the much-mourned spinner, what are their roles on the contemporary Championship pitch? The length that the faster bowler will attempt to bowl on a good surface will be dependent on his pace (and therefore the kind of bounce he can anticipate), his action, his height and his mental make-up. If he is more inclined to attack he may be happy to invite the drive in the hope that a subtle change of pace or some slight movement off the pitch will find the batsman out. If he is content to frustrate the batsman he will want to keep him off the front foot and committed to defence. Many bowlers are considered 'unlucky' because they beat the batsman regularly without finding the outside edge. However, such apparent misfortune is often self-induced. In their concern not to concede runs, they consistently bowl to a length which is marginally too short: any movement then carries the ball past the bat or into the pad, rather than taking the edge to waiting close catchers.

A medium-pacer's ideal length on a good pitch recalls the classic definition that the best ball will be the one which leaves the batsman uncertain whether to play forward or back. Certain bowlers in the past were almost mechanical in hitting that length. Men such as Geoff Arnold or Robin Jackman, both raised on the unforgiving surfaces at the Oval, would, at their best, bowl twenty-eight balls in thirty on precisely the right spot, meaning that front-foot drives risked offering an edge and back-foot drives became too cramped. Middlesex's Angus Fraser, whose height gives him the further advantage of generating unexpected lift, would perhaps be the closest contemporary equivalent to such players.

It was instructive in 1990 to watch the enforced introduction into the Northamptonshire attack of John Hughes, a hitherto unknown local medium-pacer from Wellingborough. Injury to five fast bowling colleagues who would have gained selection ahead of him brought Hughes, at the age of 19, into the team, and it was his ill luck that his first four matches were played at the Oval, Cheltenham, Bournemouth and Chesterfield. The Oval pitch was characteristically true and firm (Surrey proceeded to make 347–2 declared); Cheltenham and Bournemouth, once turners, now provided pace for Gloucestershire's Courtney Walsh and Hampshire's Malcolm Marshall respectively; and Queen's Park at Chesterfield is consistently the fastest pitch in the country.

Hughes had played all his cricket in the Second XI on the damp, slow club surfaces of the Midlands. At the Oval, his line was entirely acceptable for a débutant, but his length, in such very different conditions, was marginally out. Over after over he was driven through an off side that was eventually populated, to little avail, with four men trying to save the single. It did not help that he had to begin his spell against two left-handed openers, Darren Bicknell and Grahame Clinton, who were both by then well on their way to big hundreds. On a true surface he continually overpitched, if only minimally, to the cruel delight of professionals who scented easy runs. In the course of his next three games, in which Northamptonshire conceded 1163 first-innings runs while securing just 22 wickets, Hughes's length was clawed back imperceptibly, inch by inch, until he was conceding not 4 runs an over but under 3, learning quietly and wholeheartedly all the time. At Chesterfield he gained his opening 3 first-class wickets.

On the same Oval pitch, and in the same conditions which brought Surrey their 347–2, Waqar Younis took what were – for three days, at least – career-best figures of 6–36. Waqar employed the same movement in the air as Northamptonshire's Mark Robinson had, but the pitch, fast enough to carry the ball sweetly on to the stroke, was not quite quick enough for Robinson's slower pace to force an error. Swinging the ball but bowling just too short a length, Robinson consistently gave the batsman time for the late adjustment which kept him out. His determination to avoid the punishment from which Hughes was learning at the other end prevented him mounting a threatening challenge: too many runs were being conceded, and so he opted for caution.

This is not to say that a dedication to control at medium pace is a purely negative approach. Batsmen who are forced to defend by containment at both ends can be frustrated into error by their inability to score in conditions where they feel they should dominate. After he has driven the batsman on to the defensive, any assistance which the bowler may extract from the pitch can then be maximised. As he seeks his minor attacking variations, the bowler will stray occasionally but, preoccupied with survival, the batsman will be less likely to profit. This bowling philosophy was one which was lost in the mid- to late 1980s because seaming pitches offered far easier paths to success. It does not follow from that, however, that the answer is to introduce the kind of sterile batting surfaces encountered in 1990.

Unerring accuracy alone does not make for the highest-calibre seam bowling, certainly not at Test level. Accuracy is the foundation upon which other skills are built, and such skills require an element of encouragement from the pitch. Test matches are usually played on harder, faster strips which enable the batsman to hit through the medium-pacer's line, and there is not the same urgency at this level to push the match along. There is a place for the tight, dogged seamer here, but it is in a support capacity. For eight years or so in the 1980s the New Zealanders, making canny use of limited resources, strategically deployed first Ewan Chatfield and, after him, Martin Snedden to hold the ground while the spearhead of Richard Hadlee or, latterly, Hadlee and Danny Morrison, rested for a fresh assault. Chatfield, in forty-three Tests, gained a wicket only once every 14 overs; except on the odd green New Zealand pitch, his analyses would not win matches.

An English parallel here might be Tim Tremlett who, despite 450 first-class wickets for Hampshire at only 24 runs each, never represented his country. He did, however, tour Sri Lanka with an England B side in 1985–86 and found patient batsmen and dead pitches impervious to his miserly control. Had Tremlett been a New Zealander he might conceivably have gained fifteen Test caps – within a very specific, strategic role. Yet men like Tremlett

– or Paul Allott and Yorkshire's Arnie Sidebottom among his direct contemporaries – had more to their armouries than a command of length and line. Even on pitches which leaned to the bat any limited assistance would be fully exploited.

While medium-pacers should not be given pitches upon which they can bowl out sides for under 200, neither should they be denied all hope. Otherwise the result in Championship cricket becomes all too predictable: containment, less as a positive element in the search for wickets than as a matter of damage-limitation in the one-day mould. Far from fostering a new Alec Bedser or Maurice Tate, you promote a cynical manipulation of the three-day format: batsmen, needing bonus points, are invited to self-destruct and matches, ticking over, simply await the final-day run chase.

If the argument is that by refusing him significant assistance, you force the bowler to become more inventive, then the fate of the spinner seems to disprove it. The battle between batsman and spinner on slow and unhelpful surfaces – surfaces upon which the ball will not bite, turn or bounce – is not so much an even contest as an attempted assassination. The negative frame of mind which has developed among spinners is now almost universal in the Championship game. Bishan Bedi's claim in his six seasons at Northampton in the 1970s was that the single basic necessity for the slow bowler is that he should be able to spin the ball. That anything so obvious should now smack of wisdom may indicate the true extent of the spinner's privation. Bedi meant that the player must first learn how to spin the ball and then work at marrying this to control. One-day bowling and the repeated containment of batsmen attempting to force the pace in the Championship have reversed this thinking completely.

There is an absolute difference in attitude and intent between attacking spin bowling which wins matches and defensive slow bowling which seeks to undo the batsman who goes too far. Today, the former will be seen perhaps ten times at most in 187 Championship games a season. Perhaps Surrey's Keith Medlycott is the only contemporary Championship cricketer who would wholly fulfil Bedi's criterion of spin, and he is an expensive bowler in terms of runs per over for that very reason.

At the age of 26, Medlycott has many seasons ahead of him in which to find greater accuracy. In present Championship conditions, however, it would be easier for him to sacrifice genuine turn for the sake of economy. So few pitches will in fact reward spin that the attraction of such pragmatism is strong.

In the case of Northamptonshire's Nick Cook, year by year he finishes high up in the seam-dominated Championship averages as a skilful exponent of the art of taking first-innings wickets on unresponsive pitches by minute variations of flight, line, length and pace. Very few batsmen who seek to maintain the momentum towards bonus points will take more than two or three liberties against Cook before paying the penalty, and it is rare for him to start a spell with anything other than a maiden. In a run chase, however, on a pitch which is taking slow turn, Cook will seldom break through against a side fighting for a draw. When 7 wickets have fallen, for example, and the tail opts to play out a dozen overs to the close, he would not ordinarily win the match.

When Nick Cook finds the edge, it will almost certainly not carry. In six seasons bowling at Northampton, the number of his dismissals caught at slip could be counted in single figures, yet this is only a more severe form of an affliction common to most Championship bowlers. Comment is frequently passed upon the excellence of Australian slips, but what is not appreciated is how much more confidence-building their apprenticeships have been. The ball comes through consistently in Australia and enables the slips to stand upright. In England they have to crouch and are inclined to jerk up too soon; they misread the angle of a catch which is going not to midriff but to shin. This reveals much about the nature of English pitches and illustrates further the austerity of the spinner's lot. Unless slow men gain genuine encouragement from a surface in terms of bounce and speed of turn, they cannot realistically be expected to develop into the category once recognised as spin bowlers.

When Nick Cook was selected for the final three Tests of England's disastrous Ashes series in 1989, his 3–91 from 40 overs at Trent Bridge (the top three in the order, two stumped,

in a total of 602–6 declared) was one of the best analyses those
three games produced. Yet the strength of disappointment in
his flat, defensive style in media commentary was bewildering.
It was as if those who berated Cook's low trajectory and
absence of spin had not seen a Championship match in the
last ten years. To believe that spin bowling may yet revive
unaided is little more than an act of faith; certainly it is
contrary to all that the spinner's present predicament suggests.
With perhaps a dozen of proven stature left in the game, it is
difficult to see how they will escape following leg-break bowlers
into extinction.

This would be such a loss to cricket that it is astounding
how little has been done to prevent it. The glory of the contest
between a batsman and a spinner on a turning pitch lies in
the number of different methods which can be applied on
either side to achieve dominance. Where Keith Fletcher, for
example, would move calmly back on to his stumps to play
the ball from the pitch, Allan Border will use speed of foot
to bring a positive sense of purpose even to defence. For Mike
Gatting, the attitude of mind is of absolute importance: he
determines that he alone will dictate the terms of engagement, as though to show any indecision were itself to lose the
battle.

From the spinner's point of view his approach will be equally
personal. Northamptonshire's Richard Williams, for example,
will bowl to a totally different length to Middlesex's John
Emburey, to the extent of a metre and a half. Williams, flighting
the ball from his own limited height, wants a batsman to be
reaching out for it, believing he can come forward to drive. But
what in the air seems to be a half-volley proves, with its looping
trajectory, to be too short for the shot, and the result will be
an edge or a lofted shot to mid-on or mid-off. In contrast,
Emburey will bowl flat to a far shorter length, gaining extra
bounce from his height and seeking to keep the batsman ever
defensive in his crease. He harasses where Williams blandishes,
telling the batsman he cannot play as Williams suggests he
might try.

The gulf between two players nominally exercising the same
craft, and certainly seeking the same end, might stand for

Championship cricket itself. In such commonplace observations, perhaps, is found the historic appeal of the game. The psychology of the dispute between spinner and batsman is as subtle and compulsive as exists in the game; that it is also endangered by change speaks of the world in which cricket is played.

FIVE

Test Match Cricket

Throughout the course of the last few seasons, almost the whole of professional thinking in the English game has turned towards finding an ultimate aim which might bring purpose and definition to the daily practice of domestic cricket. The process has resulted not only in a desire for a successful England team, but in the ever more explicitly stated belief that a successful England team holds the key to the game's future. Significant changes have accordingly taken place in the organisation of county cricket. We have seen the introduction of four-day matches, a limitation on overseas players, an emphasis on 'good' playing surfaces, the relative redirection of finance to Test needs, an encouragement of representative international matches below full England level and an insistence on preparation both for home Test teams and for winter touring parties.

The list is not exhaustive, but it is sufficiently lengthy to indicate that, despite continued reticence over further alterations notably to the programme of one-day cricket, a major shift in perspective has come about. This is geared towards creating a Test side which can attract the support of both public and sponsor, and it is informed by the theory that it is Test performance above all which dictates the health of the game at other levels. To the majority of professional players, the cricket thinking behind the argument is both broadly sound and for the most part welcome; but this has been so for a number of years. The urgency which has most recently communicated itself to the counties has been born of a fear of imminent financial difficulty.

County cricket has become a high-cost enterprise reliant upon sponsorship and the sale of hospitality boxes to sustain both development and the search for success. The pursuit of outside sources of revenue, additional to inadequate gate and membership returns, was in the beginning a matter of inevitability if counties were to overcome their near-bankruptcy at the end of the 1960s. Once embraced, however, commercial involvement carries a momentum of its own: for counties to attract good players and expand facilities so they can compete on the field, they are at least committed to maintaining present levels of real income. It became increasingly obvious in the mid-1980s that this would not be possible in the long term; the prospect was for a serious drop in revenue unless something restored fresh vigour to the game. Counties began to realise that, for cricket to be attractive either to sponsors or for business entertainment, it had to maintain consistent prominence in the public's awareness and interest. The belief has consequently grown that the level of popular affection for cricket, and with it a club's ability to market the game, relates directly to Test success.

In the euphoria of the impossible Ashes victory in 1981 it seemed unthinkable that English cricket could decline so rapidly or that the warmth of popular endearment could so soon fade. It was not quite grasped at the time how critical was the influence of Ian Botham not only for England's success, but for the ardent levels of support which the game attracted. For a time the Test attack was largely built around his astonishing fervour and strike rate, concealing future deficiencies. By the middle of the decade, however, a growing lethargy began to afflict both Test thinking and performance. Despite victories home and abroad against Australia, England lost the two 1986 half-series to India and New Zealand, an outcome inconceivable in any previous era, and for the first time at home a series against Pakistan was lost in 1987. With each successive defeat even the possibility of revival seemed to become more remote; self-confidence and the will to win had apparently disappeared.

This was matched by what county cricketers saw as a complete stagnation of the selection process. Incumbent Test players, it seemed, were retained less for their ability than from an ignorance of other candidates who might at least bring enthusiasm and zest to the side. The confidence of the professionals was further eroded when, as if the custodians of Test cricket were demonstrating that they were in touch after all, four different captains were employed during the 1988 visit of the West Indies. Although a new management regime had been installed by the following summer, the structure had neither fully crystallised nor begun to implement its plans before England had so humiliatingly lost the Ashes in 1989. It was a series undermined by continuous secret negotiation over another illicit tour of South Africa, a recurrent theme in England's decline in the 1980s, which detracted further from the side's sense of purpose and, subconsciously, from its level of commitment.

There have been prolonged periods of disappointment and failure many times in England's Test history. The 1980s were characterised, however, by a sense of default on the part of the county clubs, preoccupied by a zeal for local success even where the means to this end were to the detriment of Test performance. It amounted to an abdication of responsibility for the national game. Rather than taking a decisive lead when the signs of paralysis became clear, county clubs needed the Test results of 1988 and 1989 to make them alive to fears for the immediate future. The low esteem in which cricket was held was in danger of becoming critical.

At the same time the defections to South African rebel cricket in 1989–90 presented the England management with an opportunity it would otherwise have lacked. Proposals for innovation and credible long-term planning gained new degrees of urgent support at county level. Unencumbered by any realistic expectation of success on the Caribbean tour of 1989–90, the captain and team manager assembled an untried, almost novice England party, into which was instilled a strong sense of determination and pride in performance. The rigour of the squad's preparation, assisted by an unparalleled, structured use of specialist help and advice, lent further weight to the impression that new directions were being sought.

The handful of encouraging performances which have occurred since the England party's departure for the West Indies in January 1990 must not be allowed to overshadow the evident, if overstated, problems apparent in Australia in 1990–91 and the continuing, untreated problems in the domestic game. Yet the change of direction brings England thinking better into line with the outlook which has long prevailed among the players, that is, that it is essential for international cricketers to be sufficiently prepared and sincerely enough regarded if they are to give of their best for England. For most cricketers the driving force in their careers is the hope of representing their country; without the prospect of testing themselves against the very best, their dedication to cricket would lack meaning. Some of the force of this assertion may have been diminished by the readiness of a few cricketers of limited Test experience to trade this aspiration for South African money, but for the great majority Test cricket retains its resonance.

Continuity of both selection policy and international planning has long been the demand of professionals. England's management must guard against allowing their welcome commitment to these aims to breed any feeling of exclusivity; while promoting excellence and a squad mentality at the top, contact with the rest of the game cannot be diminished. The England manager is quite rightly a figure of real stature in the running of cricket at all levels, and it is important that the two sides of his job should have equal emphasis: as he develops a nucleus of talent for the Test team, so he must ensure the best conditions for growth in the nursery.

As Test cricket has been reorganised, selection is now in the hands of three paid individuals: the chairman of the selectors, the England manager and the Test captain. A power of veto from a representative of the TCCB was revealed over the alleged unsuitability of Mike Gatting, the nominated England captain for the 1989 Ashes series. That notorious intervention occurred, however, when the management structure was in its infancy; it is highly doubtful that conflict of this kind will arise again. The dismissal and selection of either chairman or manager remains in the hands of the TCCB; should its cricket committee judge that progress has not been made it will be its prerogative to make changes. On a daily basis, however, responsibility lies with the immediate management, specifically with the manager and captain who are in charge from the moment players are assembled for a home Test and for the length of an overseas tour, both in preparation and play. Given this greater involvement, they also enjoy a decisive influence in selection; since they are responsible for the formulation of short-term and long-term strategies it is only right they should be given the players they want to carry these strategies out.

There is also now a place for consultation in the selection procedure and, to tackle the acknowledged problem of the management's detachment from the county game, certain observers were appointed to watch Championship play in the various regions of England. They were also asked to cultivate a network of contacts – umpires, captains and respected professionals, for example – who could be regularly sounded out for advice. Some counties report they are very familiar with their observer (presently the appointees are Alan Knott, Phil Sharpe and Fred Titmus); others claim never to have seen him, presumably because he feels he will be unwelcome. Yet it is important that this system should be seen to work, because the game was grateful for the indication that the England management had become amenable to constructive criticism. To date, confidence remains fairly high that consistent decisions are being made.

The centrality of the captain's role in fashioning the identity of a team is qualified at Test level by the need for the captain to be worth his place by virtue of the runs and/or wickets he contributes. There are exceptions to this: Mike Brearley is always cited, although, for a batsman of his ability, it was a surprise that he failed to make more consistent scores. A better example, perhaps, is Ray Illingworth in that the innings he played in adversity were an unexpected bonus for the selectors who appointed him. Such exceptions aside, the emphasis on captaincy cannot be so strong in Tests as it is in the county game. Very few cricketers in any generation will be assured of a regular Test place, and the choice of captain is therefore necessarily more constrained. As a general principle, however, if selectors can identify a player as a near-certain starter for the next three or four years, it would be sound to appoint him captain. This has been a position more usually adopted abroad (one thinks of Allan Border, Viv Richards and the steady New Zealand sequence of Geoff Howarth, Jeremy Coney and John Wright) than in England.

The only problem which this approach can promote, the more so under England's present structure, is that the question of a successor is put off and the captain becomes almost too integral to a side's success. Possibly reflecting the peculiar circumstances under which Graham Gooch moulded a virtually new team by the strength of his own personality in the heat of the 1989–90 West Indies tour, there was then a hint of demoralisation in the England camp when the captain was injured, both in the Caribbean and in Australia the following winter. These, though, are not insuperable difficulties; if the management takes account of the dangers, continuity of captaincy should remain the ideal.

When Geoff Cook played his first home Test, his captain, Bob Willis, offered an observation which at the time seemed unnecessary: 'The biggest difference between Test and county cricket is the fact that it is five days as opposed to three.' Only with some experience of the game did the wisdom of this apparently obvious point become clear. The dimension of time is probably the single most important element in the distinctiveness of all cricket, but from the five-day structure of a Test match flow so many of its essential features and demands.

Precisely because of the length of time involved, a period of unforced error, or of failure to take advantage of helpful circumstances, is far more likely to be regretted. The comparative shortness of playing time in the Championship enables a side to salvage situations more swiftly and with less effort. There, when the opposition lack time to force victory, to retain a chance of winning they must allow the opponents back into the match. Such gambles have little part in Test cricket: if the other side cannot be made to submit they can at least be made to suffer. It is this attitude which dictates, on the one hand, the mental strength and tenacity to survive long sessions in adversity and, on the other, a heightened alertness to the need to punish shortcomings when the advantage moves only marginally in your favour.

Where both teams have mastered this approach it can lead, as its best, to a sense of each side stalking the other, relentlessly watching for any hint of vulnerability. This, perhaps, is the game's essence: very good players performing to their limit in such a highly exposed environment that, if the teams are of equal ability, it is the stronger willed one which succeeds. For more assured exhibitions of exhilarating talent, three-day cricket is probably the safer bet; Tests carry no guarantee of the spectacle they can sometimes produce. Given the attritional, manoeuvring, even defensive frame of mind which is brought to bear, there is always the prospect not of a sustained combat of wits, but of descent into stalemate. Often this is associated with paceless or flat pitches. Rightly, however, greater care attends the preparation of Test surfaces; since the best players are performing, they have a right to expect the best conditions. If conditions are inferior they detract from the very notion of Tests as contests between the highest levels of excellence in the cricket of two nations.

Where changes of innings do not coincide with intervals, uninterrupted Tests now involve a minimum of 446 overs in the full five days; the three-day Championship match needs 313. Thus Test matches, if they achieve the ICC's stipulation of fifteen overs per hour, are 43 per cent longer than three-day games but only 6 per cent longer than four-day games. Though the figures point to a blurring of the time distinction, through a potentially disastrous tendency to slow over rates down, the discrepancy may still make a significant difference. The full distinction, however, is not only in time, but in the quality and significance of each ball bowled. In a Test match, rather than striking for victory in the bold dash, you first deny the opposition the ascendant and then build slowly from the advantage secured. If the opponent fights for every inch of ground, the game is long enough to keep alive the lurking threat of revival: the advantage gained, therefore, can rarely be thought unassailable. At the same time, the game is also too long for catastrophic failure to be left unpunished. Both factors mean that any mental and emotional relaxation will be penalised.

The emphasis, then, is on the pace of the game, a pace which lends heightened importance to every ball bowled and to the ability to assess what is happening around you. The requisite balance is between maintaining a concentrated vigilance and yet still playing without inhibition – not quite the same approach as that conveyed in the unhelpful advice to 'play your natural game'. A player's game must be natural in that it should not alter technically, but style and approach are always tempered by the confines and requirements of a new situation. The 'natural game', after all, is the one which has been appropriate to three-day success, and a Test is not a three-day game.

Bob Willis always felt less burdened as England captain when Chris Tavaré was in his side because he brought a feeling of permanence to the batting line-up. As a bowling captain Willis could relax in the dressing-room, knowing that if Tavaré became established he would bat all day. In so doing, of course, he was closing the opposition out of the contest, which in most circumstances in a Test is precisely what you are seeking to do. The point is to avoid being physically impeded in your allotted role; you do not, for example, play a stroke in a different or indecisive way or change your action in mid-game, but you do analyse what is required and, as positively as in three-day cricket, apply yourself to the necessary task.

In practice, the Test-match mentality creates certain familiar features. Bowlers tend to be more tightly aggressive and are supported by more attacking fields which are retained for longer periods of time. Batsmen are more wary, more solid in defence and more alert to the bad ball. The characteristic commitment is to the gradual wresting of the initiative. Tactics in Test matches are accordingly far more stereotyped and, indeed, far easier to devise. Invention is not only less evident, it is less necessary: since ordinarily you are as concerned to avoid defeat as you are to win, the incentive to take risks is reduced.

With the advent of the emphasis on fast bowling this tactical uniformity has become more pronounced. There is very little subtlety in the West Indies' strategy of short-of-a-length fast bowling supported by an ever-present cordon of slips, and this approach has been imitated almost universally, albeit by altogether less hostile attacks. If other countries lack the West Indies' resources of ability and speed, they nevertheless commit themselves to batteries of quick bowlers who place similar emphasis on denial and constriction, and also seek the accompanying security of depth in batting. While the exception to this has long been Pakistan, whose bowlers bring diverse levels of skill to the game, preventing tactical rigidity, Test-match theory is often a rather meagre field.

In turn, over rates have drifted down to render the game less tactically demanding; the fewer deliveries you bowl, the easier it becomes to deny the opposition their chance of getting ahead, and the less runs you concede. It can, of course, be argued that this largely unconscious slide into safety-first thinking is counter-productive; the opportunity to take wickets, after all, is equally reduced. However, the premise with which a match starts is not solely, or even predominantly, that a Test is there to be won. In a waiting game, over rates will only increase when the bowling side feels it is clearly on top and needs to force its advantage home.

There is nothing inherently wrong with this hard, uncompromising philosophy; it can create rivetingly competitive cricket. It is when time-wasting cheats the better team and allows the consequences of error to be evaded that an immense threat appears, and the game risks becoming totally without point. If over rates are allowed to slow right down the effect will be to moderate the atmosphere of heightened tension and difficulty which is distinctive of Tests. If a rate of only twelve overs an hour is maintained through a five-day Test, one side must find in effect no more than 500 runs in the course of two completed innings to gain at least the draw, and the idea of Test cricket as an examination of attitude as well as of skill begins to recede.

It is important to emphasise that the West Indies' strategy was not conceived to avoid defeat. Far from it: in the last dozen years, the side has gained a greater percentage of Test victories than any other country. Nor is it the case that, in West Indian hands, a reliance on slow over rates has deterred the crowds; all Test-match attendances are in decline, but the West Indies remain the leading attraction. Moreover, neither element of the fast bowling/slow over rate amalgam is a West Indian invention: England's use of bodyline in 1932–33 and of delaying tactics in 1954–55 are established precedents. The point is that, although the strategy brings victory and is apparently appealing to new audiences, it makes Test cricket predictable and monolithic. Whatever its fascination, it owes nothing to a conception of the game as a profound interplay of separate themes, and great bowlers of massive cricketing intelligence and talent have, to a degree, been wasted; men like Malcolm Marshall, Andy Roberts and Michael Holding were so very rarely seen to the fullest breadth of their prodigious ability.

Test cricket has changed in every era; who, then, has the right to dictate its form? There comes a point when the answer lies with the people who fail to watch it. The problem is more dangerously acute elsewhere, but even in England crowd figures have fallen. In the hands of emulators who lack the firepower to use it properly, the West Indian method of slowing the match down can only mean embracing the draw. The trait is not yet general, but the warnings are quite clear: declining over rates are a critical threat to the international game. If it is acceptable to drop to 13 overs an hour, why not 12 or 11, or even single figures? Such conditions, after all, offer the tantalising vision of a common security from defeat.

If Test cricket is to be worthy of the name, then, minimum over stipulations have to be enforced. At the very least the present rates of 15 overs per hour, bowled within a defined day's play, must be maintained at pain of the most stringent fines. There is an obligation here for national boards of control to ensure that these fines are not paid by mysterious outside sponsors, but by the players themselves. Yet the problem is not to indicate solutions, but to realise why solutions are forever retarded. The sectionalism and self-interest within the International Cricket Conference, the ruling body of Test cricket, rather mirrors that of English cricket in the mid-1980s. In England, financial constraints ultimately compelled a concern for Test standards; it is to be hoped that the financial implications of what, outside England, are truly alarming falls in Test attendances will prompt international action before it is too late.

The key questions in Test cricket are ultimately far more personal than those of tactics: how easy is the individual adjustment both to differences in play and to the emotional strain which Test cricket involves; and why do so few players effect a successful transition? Geoff Cook played seven times for England and went on two overseas tours, to India and Sri Lanka in 1981–82 and Australia the following winter. He made his Test début in Sri Lanka's inaugural Test in Colombo in February 1982, played the three matches of India's series in England that summer and three further matches during Bob Willis's unsuccessful defence of the Ashes. The last of his caps was won in Sydney in January 1983. His entire Test career encompassed 325 days, 122 more than the number of runs he made in thirteen innings.

On being introduced to Test cricket he found it very difficult to take in the subtle changes in pace and emphasis. He felt that all he wanted to do was to have the chance to get on the field and bat as he thought he could bat. When he finally had the opportunity to reflect on what was needed in Test cricket, on how hidden, and in some cases how obvious, the changes were, it was too late; but he deeply wanted to have a chance of another crack at it after that period of reflection. If a cricketer who had by then captained his county for three seasons still found difficulty in reaching even a provisional assessment of what exactly Test matches required, then the predominant response of younger débutants must be close to bewilderment.

To become fully integrated into the Test system and adequately grasp its implications requires a period of as long as eighteen months; by today's international calendar this might involve an extended run of up to fifteen matches. It is hardly surprising, then, that so few Test players ever fulfil what is classified as 'promise'. England's selection policy has only just begun to reflect a view which has always been more respected abroad: if those selecting a side have faith in their own judgement, then a young player should be given long enough to prove them right or wrong. Even so, it remains almost inconceivable that an England player could be allowed a sequence of even five Tests, far less fifteen, without contributing two or three performances of note. Yet the aggregate achievement of, say, four different players selected to fill the same role through fifteen Tests is likely to be less impressive than that of one single player who has been given the confidence of an assured run.

If in eighteen months a player has failed to show consistent progress, it is probably true that he lacks the ability, either cricketing or mental, to offer more than an eligible rival. Justice then demands that another should have his chance. From the pool of available talent in the English game, perhaps five to seven players in most seasons will, by near-universal consensus, be far superior to their peers. For the remaining places in the Test side as many as fifteen to twenty other cricketers will have their firm advocates, and matching these candidates to an ideal is always a matter of compromise. Selection will rest on percentages not absolutes, using the criteria of ability, extended good form, mental stability, commitment and cricketing intelligence; the team's strategy and philosophy here will be important and will influence the relative weight attached to each of these factors.

The process of selection can hardly be undertaken as a pastime, but calls for knowledge, considerable evidence and, most importantly, complete confidence in your own fitness to judge. A great deal of the debate outside a selection committee will be ill-informed and partial; if an England player fails in even two Test matches, especially at home, 'public opinion' – by which is effectivcly meant the press, radio and television – will begin to demand he is dropped. Yet the professional player, striving in Test cricket for the ultimate validation of his career, has a right to expect that this criticism will be discounted. Too often, however, selection has been compliant with ignorance.

If England's selectorial policy has at last recognised the virtues of stability, the victims of its recent past are innumerable, although one illustration can stand for many. Since the properties of a potential Test opener might be unflappability, correctness and organisation in style, the ability to bat for long periods and a career average of 40, then Kent's Mark Benson would seem a most appropriate candidate. The point here is not whether this attempted matching of man to role is considered accurate or not: Benson *was* chosen and chosen before others, but was then discarded after a single appearance. What hitherto unknown flaw could this one appearance possibly have revealed? Geoff Cook's own experiences lead him to believe that to succeed in Test cricket you have to be either very good, very able mentally or to have your limitations in ability compensated for by imperviousness to criticism and to the pressure generated by the occasion; that is, to possess real strength of character.

During the Ashes tour of 1982–83, Lancashire's Graeme Fowler, then with one cap, was Cook's immediate rival for the opening position with Tavaré. Fowler was having the most wretched time of his life on tour and could hardly get a run; his game had fallen apart and his confidence had disintegrated. It was so bad that he was bowled by Trevor Chappell while ducking a full toss – probably the absolute rock bottom of

his career. On the morning of the second Test, when Cook
had to pull out through injury, Fowler suddenly found that
he was going to open the batting. He made only a few in the
first innings, but in the second he scored probably the most
courageous 83 runs he would ever score in his life, staying at
the crease for six hours while constantly playing and missing
outside his off stump against quality fast bowling from Geoff
Lawson, Carl Rackemann and Jeff Thomson. Totally out of
touch, barracked by the crowd and abused by his opponents, he
displayed a quite vast strength of mind. Reports of that innings
spoke of Fowler 'riding his luck'. This is what is meant by
an imperviousness not only to your own inabilities, but to the
criticism, from all sides, which would have them magnified.

Although it is a commonplace that the step up into international cricket involves a severe test of personality and nerve,
the terms 'tension', 'pressure', and particularly 'temperament'
need to be examined further. Geoff Cook recalls that from the
moment he walked through the gate at the start of a Test
match he realised he was in for something different. There
is a whole general hubbub about the occasion that is never
apparent apart from perhaps in a one-day final – but those
finals have an element of razzamatazz that is not present in a
Test match. The preparation of the other players also conveys
this distinctiveness. From a look in the eye or a tautness of
feature it is evident that the intensity which marks the match
is of a degree unknown before. It can indeed become an ordeal,
a relentless examination; it will be satisfying, if you can survive
and display your aptitude for cricket; but for most it will hardly
be pleasurable.

Coming into a county's first team from the Second XI is the
greatest leap in a player's career, but the difference is in terms
of skill and the range of understanding which must eventually
be mastered. At Test level the adjustment is to determination,
passion and, indeed, aggression: it is less a question of the
ability of the opponent than of his desire to defeat you. There
is an extent to which the skills which have served a Second XI
player are no longer appropriate to him at full county level. In a
Test there is no such adaptation of technique; the same skills are
employed as at county level, in a more expert and concentrated

form, but the unremitting intensity of combat has no parallel in the daily county programme.

Geoff Cook found that he enjoyed all the peripheral activities of the Test match – the pre-match dinner, the players getting together and talking about the county matches they had just left, and so on. But once the realisation hit him that the game was not far away, the atmosphere became very oppressive and, in many respects, a shade overpowering. There is little which can be done in advance of a match to prepare for this experience, one which will be unique for the newcomer however much cricket he has played. It will involve degrees of emotional and mental strain which, although they can be described, cannot be simulated. The team management can lend a certain security with consistent selection policies and a readiness to explain their thinking; they can assure the player that his ability is valued and shield him from vain expectations. In terms of coping with the occasion itself, however, it will be a matter for the individual alone.

It is not even as if the experience will necessarily become easier through repeated contact. Geoff Cook remembers talking one day on tour to Geoff Miller, a man who had already played thirty Tests by then. The two shared a room, and Miller was just lolling around when Cook tried to gee him up and get him out to enjoy himself. 'Enjoyment,' he said, 'it's got nothing to do with enjoyment. I just can't stand the whole concept of Test cricket.' This did not mean that he could not play it or that he did not want to play it. But he said that every ball he bowled or faced was a nightmare for him, although he performed again and again with sufficient distinction to remain in the side for nearly six years. Yorkshire's John Hampshire, whose introduction could not have been more encouraging in that he remains the only man to have scored a century at Lord's on his England début, against West Indies in 1969, nevertheless felt an equally forbidding anticipation as each subsequent Test drew near. It is a sense of dread which stays with him still as an umpire, although it tends to pass now when the game begins.

If part of the stress stems from being the object of group hostility, it is hardly surprising that the pressure is often as heavy upon officials as it is upon players. Umpire Barry Meyer was taken off the international list for a period in the early

1980s because it was felt that his skill had been undermined by constant high exposure. In Geoff Cook's home début, against India at Lord's in 1982, he was given out by Meyer in circumstances sufficiently unclear for the scoreboard to record the dismissal wrongly as caught behind. In the end Meyer took the unusual step of walking across to the scoreboard operators to correct this to lbw. As a result of the incident, he was subjected to such later scrutiny that he began to develop a self-consciousness which affected his highly-rated ability.

The damage to Meyer's self-confidence here was unintentional, although there are times when Test teams are guilty of trying to induce it quite deliberately, as an extension of what they are attempting to inflict upon their opponents. There is at least some degree to which Test cricket entails the wilful pursuit of humiliation, a desire to uncover insecurity in the opponent which amounts almost to an attack on his right to be called a cricketer. The affection in which Meyer is held in the game flows very much from those qualities of sensitivity and reserve which, unwittingly, were probed here as weaknesses.

When this process manifests itself in certain ways between players it is sometimes held to offend the spirit of the game. Yet actual verbal abuse on the field is probably no more than the literal expression of what is being sought more covertly. For an Englishman, with an immediate background of English Championship cricket, the experience of the game in Australia is something of a shock. Australians (and to a large extent South Africans) probably adjust to the Test-match stage more readily and more quickly, bringing to bear a competitiveness and a mental toughness which almost certainly comes more from their culture's assertiveness than from anything specific to their cricket. In its attitudes, its lifestyles and, indeed, in its very urban skylines, Australia is now far more like the United States than Britain. It is not an accident that counties have turned to Australians and South Africans as cricket managers.

For a period in Australian cricket, the latent psychology of the Test match carried over into the kind of direct enmity which, on the 1982–83 tour, was for Geoff Cook quite startling. He expected it from the bowlers, but when he stood in close-catching positions at short-leg or silly-point, he was quite alarmed by how aggressive even the batsmen were towards the fielding team. He considered that this determination and almost complete lack of respect for the occasion meant that they were playing a totally different game to him. The Australians had a very competitive team, with players such as Greg Chappell, Kim Hughes, Graeme Wood, Kepler Wessels – and John Dyson, who took the initiative straight away, not as an aggressive batsman in his play, but as a very aggressive man. This assertion of authority in such an obviously menacing way was, to Cook, quite remarkable. It should be said that, uncompromising though Allan Border's present side is, antipathy quite so unashamedly naked as this is not associated with current Australian teams.

Once again, it is remarkable the degree to which cricket takes its metaphors from conflict. Although a lot could undoubtedly be read into this, it need indicate no more than an obvious truth. Whatever else cricket may be, it is rooted in conflict between two opposing forces. The question then is, 'Is it really worth the fight?'; does Test cricket encourage attitudes of mind which it is not altogether discreditable to lack?

The answer to that can only lie in the game itself, both for participant and onlooker. If Test matches can still offer profound, consuming interest then they will indeed be worth playing. Conflict on the Test field is not a question of actual hatred; that a team's search for control over the game, the adversary and time itself could ever bring real violence is still thought appalling. From an individual point of view, Geoff Cook found that he simply became frustrated with himself for not being able to compete in these surroundings, while recognising at the same time that Test cricket was a marvellous thing and that success in it must have given the greatest satisfaction to many people over the years. In Australia in 1982–83, he failed to get any runs in the first Test in Perth but then began to play reasonably well and scored 99 and 73 against New South Wales in the interim before the next Test. Then immediately before the second Test he got hit in the nets and broke a rib – and somewhere deep down there was a feeling of relief that he had to pull out of a Test match. It was a terrible admission to make, but was nonetheless an indication of how the game had affected him; it was a feeling he had never encountered in England, not even in a one-day final. It was simply the enormity of Test cricket in Australia.

The Australian example is extreme, as would be a Test against the West Indies today. For all professional cricketers, however, such matches remain the truest touchstones, and it is accepted that Test cricket is as it is. It would be inexcusable for a county player to claim that his failure was justifiable by pleading that the opposition were the strongest in the country and playing hard in pursuit of a title. Equally, no professional can claim that the newness of Test cricket, its intensity and pressure, gives him the right to fail. In exposure to Test cricket, a player learns a lot about himself which he may not view with any great pride, but he does not, for that reason, seek to evade the experience. County cricketers continue to be inspired by the hope of Test selection not because the challenge is expected to be particularly enjoyable, but because something in a career is unfulfilled if the most searching form of the game remains untasted.

Perhaps ten English cricketers in any decade will be able to claim they have made an historic impression on the game, and that their records can stand with those of the best in over 100 years of Tests. This points to the rare ability, sustained over series after series, to score runs or take wickets against the best opponents which cricket can present. If ten will genuinely and unequivocally succeed, at least four times that number will fail. It should be as pointless to present such odds as an argument against wanting to play Test cricket as it is to tell mountaineers, say, that for every five attempts to climb one of the great peaks four will founder, possibly ignominiously. In practice, a professional can be allowed only one attitude. It is not the fault of Test cricket that he fails to find it enjoyable; it is the fault of the player himself.

There are, however, some sublimely blessed players who find themselves immediately at home in Test cricket, who discover in it an emotion which goes beyond satisfaction or fulfilment and approaches joy. Certain orders of talent, and of the self-confidence such talent has bred, will relate immediately to the fact that Test cricket is the pinnacle of the game and as such the most fitting of contexts for the exhibition of their skill. In recent years in England this has been true pre-eminently of

Ian Botham, while David Gower's comparative records would seem to suggest that he is so much at home in Test cricket that he finds it difficult to lift himself elsewhere. Most professional cricketers regarding such players will stand almost disbelieving, in awe both of their talent and their assurance.

Yet even for these men immediate or consistent success is not guaranteed and is certainly not easy. Only a truly great ability will eventually deny the fear of the occasion any significant place in the player's mind. If he has sufficient confidence, conscious or unconscious, in his own talent, the very concept of pressure will come in the end to be regularly disarmed. It is perhaps accurate to say, then, that the truly outstanding ability will always in the last analysis confirm itself. If this can be related to the problems of selection, those of exceptional innate talent will have been both recognised and persevered with even through failure.

Cricket does not really know, then, to any tragic measure, the theme of the unfulfilled genius. The nearest thing to it in contemporary Test cricket is perhaps the New Zealand batsman, Ken Rutherford, who in Shell Trophy cricket is thought to be the most naturally capable batsman, after Martin Crowe, to have emerged in the last ten years. Despite his making over twenty Test appearances, however, little sustained evidence of his talent has yet been seen.

It is a predicament reminiscent of Mike Gatting's early Test career. In Championship cricket Gatting inspired that same degree of awed respect from his fellow professionals reserved for exceptional talent alone, but it was not until he was 27 that he achieved his first Test century. It would have been inconceivable to his colleagues that so formidable a self-belief as Gatting's could be upset by the menace of Test cricket, but his problem owed far more to living with the very levels of expectation that his apparently ideal temperament generated. As the wait for consistent runs grew longer, so eventual success became more difficult for the player to imagine. The indelible images of that period in Gatting's career are the sequence of lbw dismissals he invited when padding up and failing to offer a shot. Such basic errors from a batsman so gifted are possibly the prime recent examples of tension denying ability its expression; Gatting had begun to bat not by his own standards of cricketing intelligence, but to a subconscious, theoretical version of how the watchful Test game should be played. It is all the more to his credit, therefore, that he came through such a time of crisis and eventually confirmed his talent.

The combination of ability and the confidence gained from regular, authoritative Championship performance does not therefore guarantee immediate Test success. When Neil Fairbrother came into the England side in 1990 it seemed that his undoing owed less to any tension in his play than to his very impetuosity. He returned to the side having achieved 696 runs in five completed Championship innings at the start of the season, 366 of these coming in one celebrated performance at the Oval. Few professionals would claim that Fairbrother has quite the exceptional ability of those for whom a successful Test career seems certain, but at the time nobody was felt to be in more fluent command. He was, of course, subject to all the endemic pressures of Test cricket described above, but, more than this, there seemed to be something in his approach which illustrated again the limitations in the idea of 'playing your natural game'.

In effect, Fairbrother failed to give himself time to understand the New Zealand attack before seeking to impose his will upon it – as he had been doing with such astonishing success against county bowlers in the opening weeks of the summer. He merely underlined the need in international cricket for the batsman to analyse both the quality of the opposing attack and the context of his innings, as, correspondingly, the bowler needs to assess the style and intent of the batsman facing him and remain alert to the balance of power in the match. At Test level any deficiencies in reading cricket are so much more prone to detection because the players seeking to defeat you are able to ally their grasp of the game to the skill which can make this count. Most amateur England selectors around the county grounds will have found the Fairbrother example instructive; few selections can have been so widely urged, few recalled batsmen so full of runs and confidence, and it was hardly possible to point to a player of similar inexperience who was any more gifted than Fairbrother. Faultless logic, however, did not bring success; and it is worth noting that Fairbrother gained but two Test chances.

If there are a favoured few who have been so graced with

talent that they can embrace Test cricket without having to draw upon vast, debilitating depths of mental toil, then the pattern of Allan Lamb's Test career might be seen almost perversely to exemplify the point. As a native South African, Lamb's need to establish a residential qualification for England meant that he did not receive his first cap until he was 26. Through the preceding four seasons for Northamptonshire nobody doubted that he had not only the very highest Test quality, but also the perfect attitude to succeed. Lamb did indeed come to the Test arena as if to his natural environment. Yet he created no great initial impact and his career became overshadowed by the strangest of anomalies. No England batsman in Test history has scored more centuries against the West Indies (a quite astounding fact given their power over the last ten years), but Lamb's Test average remained in the mid-30s.

Lamb's cricketing persona is remarkable in that nothing gives him quite the same positive enjoyment as a backs-to-the-wall fight; nobody for Northamptonshire can ever have retrieved singlehandedly so many apparently impossible situations. It is precisely this subconscious need for the challenge which is reflected in his record against weaker opposition; it is not that he has tried less hard, but that the same swell of pride and determination in adversity has failed to build up in him consistently. Interestingly, he has for some time recognised the threat that his record will not do him justice: this itself has been made the challenge with which he can approach each new Test.

SIX

One-Day Cricket

In his book *The Shining Mountain*, the late Peter Boardman described how he and Joe Tasker attempted to prepare themselves for the ascent of Changabang's West Wall. They persuaded security guards to let them sleep in the cold store of a Salford frozen-food depot. The book in consequence includes one of the more remarkable sentences a work of non-fiction can ever have contained: 'We spent another two nights in the fridge before we were satisfied.'

The exertions of one-day cricket hardly compare to those of a two-man expedition up a 4,500-foot granite face in the Garwhal Himalaya; nor, indeed, are its training schedules quite so novel. But the incorporation into the English cricket season of what for the last twenty years has been four weeks of one-day cricket (as opposed to ten weeks of 'real' cricket) has brought about a similarily 'alternative' approach to the game. Certainly when it comes to the Sunday League, the professionals play a completely different sport for their salaries: instead of one that is contemplative and intellectually taxing, this is frenetic and severely clinical in its tactical disciplines.

One-day cricket owes everything to crowds. It was conceived as a means of regaining paying customers and it expanded to save the game from bankruptcy. As its popularity was confirmed so it attracted yet further money in sponsorship and broadcasting fees. Buoyed by both factors of revenue and public esteem, it has assumed a greater practical influence on some counties than the Championship itself. The days when a Yorkshire captain, Brian Close, could publicly declare his contempt for the Sunday League, and thereby imply that his side merely went through the motions in playing it, are long gone: one-day competitions are now an immutable part of the professional programme. For players coming into the game, with a background of limited-overs cricket in clubs and the Second XI and Under-19 versions of the World Cup, one-day cricket is not even a major issue, but a settled feature of the game as they have always known it.

From all the evidence of crowd reaction at a limited-overs match it is apparent that the appeal of one-day cricket lies in the assertive, even brutal, dominance of bat over ball. This still requires a convincing context: 40-over attendances are clearly declining and the Refuge Assurance Cup of the last few seasons has failed to generate real interest. Hitting that is too patently contrived has begun to pall; but the high-scoring, quick-tempo cup matches which are long enough to make hitting a matter of risk still retain their following. The other arts of the game are entirely secondary, and may not even be noticed at all by the majority of spectators. Good catching and fielding can obviously be appreciated, but good bowling is often unrecognised in that it does not usually seek wickets. Acknowledged or not, it is a mere sideshow to the fast run-scoring and the prospect of seeing boundaries.

The prevalence of boundary-hitting in the one-day game has significantly altered the perceptions of at least some elements in a Championship crowd. Some twenty years ago the batsmen who would regularly advance their scores by a high proportion of hard-struck blows were few, and the visit of cricketers like Garry Sobers, Colin Milburn, Rohan Kanhai, Hylton Ackerman or David Green would arouse a special anticipation. One-day norms on good batting pitches now promise two or three such powerful strikers in every opposing side. It is for this reason, perhaps, and the increased partisanship which limited-overs cricket has fostered, that Dermot Reeve could come to Northampton in 1990 to score a Championship double-century for Warwickshire and attract ceaseless complaint for his pains. To certain regulars, his one-day renown simply compounded the problem; many were unable to realise that this uncharacteristically watchful innings, a career-best, was winning a four-day match for his county.

The most important element in a one-day game is the pitch. It should, as near as possible, be a batting paradise, dry throughout so that conditions remain reasonably even. There will, of course, be the possibility of dew at the start and close or of differences in light but, such variables aside, both teams will be given an equal chance of victory.

It would be unfair to say that, in these conditions, non-first-class sides will always lose, but slow, low-scoring pitches, the opposite of the above formula, do offer them a far greater chance. Not only are dull pitches more familiar to club and minor county players, but they blunt the sometimes alarming power of shot which one-day cricket has brought to the professional game. Despite – or perhaps because of – odds since 1973 of about 25/1 against humiliation, first-class cricketers carry into games against lowly opposition a certain fear of defeat. This can lead to an inhibition in their play which proves particularly debilitating if the first session maintains the balance or begins to slip away. Where 50:50 positions persist, the professionals, for all their experience of pressure, are more likely to succumb to anxiety than their opponents.

For the most part, however, both minor and first-class counties do abide by a desire to produce good, day-long spectacles of run-scoring, and they will not usually prepare pitches to disarm visiting stroke-makers or assist their own seamers to contain. If one-day games have fallen short of this ideal in the course of the last few seasons, this has reflected the lack of time now available to groundsmen, who are more concerned with the oppressive need for irreproachable Championship pitches. The desire to ensure plentiful runs and high excitement is largely dictated by the importance of major one-day ties for financial security. Economic self-interest promotes a wish to provide the greatest satisfaction so that paying customers return another day or may even become members. In that sense, there is perhaps a slight danger that the increasingly – and disturbingly – partisan nature of support on the big one-day occasion may lure counties into seeking victory above entertainment; to date, however, there is gratifyingly little evidence of such a trend.

Low-scoring games can still be just as exciting in their climaxes as any other kind of one-day match, and Sunday cricket, where the 40-over limitation makes for both low scores and the improbability of a side's dismissal, often seems to consist of thrilling finishes alone. All too frequently, the interest here is reserved for the last ten overs, the period of perhaps forty minutes before the close of the innings. The connoisseur of Championship play may perhaps enjoy the emphasis on mental attitude which tense, low-scoring one-day matches can produce; for most, however, the response to 60-over totals of, say, 200 per side will be that for up to seven hours the match has failed to come alive.

Players, too, in the main find these ties annoying. One-day cricket has so clearly become a top-order batsman's game that, without the regular punctuation of riotous applause for boundaries, the occasion is robbed of its peaks of elation. It is this intense thrill of the passing moment which makes especially knock-out cup cricket both an enjoyably different experience and, for all its nervous exhaustion, a relief from the demands of the Championship. The emotions aroused by triumph or defeat here are extreme but transitory; a player feels a much less pronounced sense of satisfaction in the days following limited-overs victories than he finds in reflecting on Championship success. Similarly, disappointment at personal failure – unless the one-day match was the season's last hope or the player's error was critical – does not last as long.

The particular technical difficulties of a one-day game derive from the tension of playing continuously against the scoreboard and in front of a big crowd without the opportunity to bat or bowl yourself into form. At the same time, however, this is all curiously less disturbing. A batsman, for example, is expected to improvise and score quickly and so his task is free of dilemma. Failure in these circumstances will be more readily excused; it will be important to the game, certainly, but in the days which follow it will soon be forgotten. Although the batsman's wicket is ordinarily dear to him, its value is considerably diminished in a one-day setting where even 25 is an acceptable score, and guilt lies less in dismissal than in falling behind the required rate of progress.

For this reason, oddly, one-day cricket can sometimes be genuinely beneficial to an out-of-form batsman. The needs of the Sunday League, for example, leave little time for self-doubt: he either scores runs or he gets out in the attempt and, crucially, few will blame him for the latter. This helps account, perhaps, for what is otherwise apparently anomalous: although he was on the way to breaking his county's Sunday League records, Worcestershire's Tim Curtis began the 1990 season with just 400 Championship runs in the first thirteen weeks. Yet his Sunday form was eventually responsible for the breaking of the dam, and Curtis went on to average 89 in twenty further innings to the summer's end.

For the participant, the relationship between one-day cricket and authentic cricket may be likened to that between a whodunnit and a 'serious' novel; the former is gripping, even stimulating, at the time, but in retrospect neither as memorable nor fulfilling as the latter. Were it a matter of mere aesthetic taste it might be unimportant that, for a long time now, clubs have tended to rest players from Championship matches in anticipation of key one-day ties – even when Championship honours were still there for the taking. In recent seasons, however, false priorities have become yet more marked, and some clubs are clearly now forming squads with a view to the one-day game alone. If this proves to be detrimental to England's Test standing, then it is undoubtedly a dangerous and reprehensible development. For it has long been a valid claim that the technical legacy of one-day cricket has been far from beneficial.

The one-day game has brought certain obvious and frequently cited gains. Improvements both in fielding and in running between the wickets have been so notable that they have on occasions materially affected the outcome of a match. Quality fielding can reduce an opponent's total by at least 25 runs, while Derbyshire's superb running arguably made the difference in 1990 between their winning the Sunday League and finishing fourth – a gap of only two tight victories.

The main dividend for batsmen is not so easily expressed in figures. There is now an awareness among players of what might be called the 'limits of the possible' with the bat. During the last twenty years, these limits have been pushed far beyond what once seemed credible, and county batsmen have gained a far wider appreciation of the spectrum of stroke-play and improvisation available to them. If the one-day game has cultivated certain shots which are perilous in 'real' cricket – the steer down wide of the wicket-keeper and through the empty slip area to third man is the usual example – it has at the same time provided an insight into what can be done to manufacture quick runs when a team has wickets in hand. In that sense, it has probably increased the overall rate of scoring in Championship cricket and perhaps even, in some circumstances at least, in Tests.

Such an increase in tempo may also have led, more harmfully, to a greater conservatism on the part of captains who carry their familiarity with one-day norms into the Championship. This means that they will go more swiftly on to the defensive or invite sides to get themselves out rather than seeking wickets. Final-day declarations in the Championship are often directed towards producing run chases which equate closely to the second innings of an extended limited-overs match; both sides may settle for the scenario which finds the chasing team attempting 200 runs in the last session of a game with 7 or 8 wickets in hand. The bowling side then anticipates capturing these wickets by allowing the one-day scheme to run its course; it knows from the limited-overs model that batsmen should periodically fall by virtue of the run rates they are attempting. This very understanding of one-day dynamics accounts for the rather bizarre fact that some teams will occasionally find it easier to score 250 in 55 overs than they will in 70. Rates of controlled acceleration in the 55-over format, especially for middle- and late-middle-order batsmen, have almost become a matter of engaging the automatic pilot: when asked to play more correctly, batsmen can prove rather more prone to uncertainty.

In batting, then, one-day blessings have been mixed. It is with the bowlers, however, that with the best will in the world it becomes impossible to identify gains. By a stretch of the analysis you could say that some have learnt to bowl yorkers more consistently; but this alone could never compensate for the magnitude of harm otherwise done. The fact is that there have been no significant benefits in bowling in terms of practical abilities which can be transferred with advantage to the three-, four- or five-day game. More to the point, limited-overs cricket has detracted appreciably from the bowler's capacity to provide sustained, probing examinations of good batsmen in authentic conditions.

The bowling needs of one-day matches are so incompatible

with the recognised technical and mental qualities required of good Championship and Test attacks that this could hardly be otherwise. It is not only a matter of bowling to contain rather than to dismiss; containment in a one-day game is a relative concept which has little to do with traditional accuracy. Equally important, the bowler has to adapt so substantially from day to day that he is not able to maintain the rhythm which comes from releasing the ball in a similar fashion every match. Since rhythm is the foundation of the bowler's art, its disruption is seriously damaging.

In any one month of the season, a bowler may play continuously the same form of cricket for, at most, two periods of six days each; the variations demanded of him by this badly hinder the realisation of his skills. Specifically, he must alter his line of attack by a distance of something approaching a foot in the separate forms of the game: in the Championship he bowls at, or just outside, the off stump; on a Sunday he slants the ball in towards middle stump to cramp a batsman who will otherwise gain room for the shot. In terms of the wrist, arm and body positions in delivery, this difference in line makes the bowler's desire to hone a smooth, second-nature action all the more difficult to achieve. Similarly, a bowler's length can change by as much as three or four yards between one-day and three-day matches, so concerned is he in the former to prevent the batsman hitting through the line of what would in the latter be termed a 'good-length' ball. For what is a good length on a Thursday morning – some four to five yards down the pitch from a batsman, to make him unsure whether to go forward or back – is a merely predictable, and therefore hittable, length in the one-day context.

For a one-day batsman driving expansively at this length, the occasional miscue is an accepted penalty of play, although his errors will more often than not fail to be found out. When a batsman ignores length in the Championship he may edge to third slip or gully, but these are precisely the fielders who will rarely be retained for very long in even a 60-over tie. It is sometimes argued that this is a tactical mistake and that slips should be kept in place longer. But one-day cricket is a batsman's game, and runs conceded in an extended pursuit of wickets will almost always be more decisive than any dismissals which such aggression might yield. When a side is bowled out in only 60 overs in the Championship, even for 260 runs, it may well face defeat by an innings; a score of this order in the NatWest Trophy keeps it in the match. The game's length, then, dictates the bowler's options: after 25 overs or so in a cup tie, and from the outset on a Sunday, his usual intent is containment alone. Twenty years ago the archetypal advice given to a young batsman on joining a county staff would have been that of Dennis Brookes, the most prolific run-maker in Northamptonshire's history: every delivery must be played on its merits, the good ball with correct defence, the bad with an appropriate means of attack. This has now altered completely. In certain situations in a one-day game, with perhaps only ten overs remaining and wickets in hand, a batsman is no longer allowed to defer to a bowler's abilities; there is no such permissible concept as 'the good ball', unless it be the yorker. The bowler's values of line and length are turned to the batsman's positive advantage; if he can predict where the next ball will pitch, he can begin to nominate shots and scoring possibilities in advance – directly counter to Brookes's classic instruction. It is at this stage that the batsman displays his standard repertoire of one-day improvisation: the run down to third man, the step away to leg to hit over the off-side infield, the move across the stumps 'outside' the ball to pull or glance to the on side, the dead-bat drop for the single to give a more established partner the strike.

Under these circumstances, certainly where batsmen have been at the crease for any length of time, it becomes almost impossible for a fielding side to contain at all. Perhaps more accurately, the definition of containment changes so utterly that conceding 'only' 6 or 7 runs an over will represent good bowling, a proposition which at most times in the orthodox game would be laughable. Unless the bowler concerned is perhaps either very quick indeed or a highly deceptive slow spinner, both the captain and the team will expect punishment and settle for the prevention of boundaries.

In this a side's attitude, its steadiness under fire, is strategically crucial. The side seeks to encourage the bowler, accepting that runs must come while attempting to abide by agreed tactics which have been designed to limit damage as fully as possible. If bowlers and fielders can hold to their tactics, and do not subside under the weight of the inevitable onslaught, they have done all that can be asked of them. These tactics may involve ensuring that the more threatening of the two batsmen – so identified because he has been at the crease longer or is innately more capable – is kept away from the strike. In the parlance which has emerged in the one-day game, the fielding side first seeks to 'get an end to bowl at' and then to make this count. It is for this reason, perhaps, that long partnerships are especially threatening in the one-day game, an even more vital factor in forging big totals than they are in the Championships.

One-day innings have a distinctly back-to-front appearance, in that not only will the number of runs in the last 15 to 20 overs often decide a match, their anticipated significance will govern a team's batting tactics in the period preceding the eruption. If the key is to have what can be called 'sacrificial' wickets in hand for the final 'thrash', a thesis now almost universally accepted, then a side needs to lose no more than three or four batsmen by varying stages of an innings: approximately overs 25, 40 and 45 respectively in the 40-, 55- and 60-over competitions.

Assuming 100 to 120 runs to be scored in the last 15 overs – given that six or seven wickets are in hand – then in a 60-over game a team wants a score of around 150–3 to 170–4 after 45 overs. Since such scores would be entirely welcome in even ten overs longer at the start of a Championship match, the degree of orthodox application needed to keep wickets in hand is high. In a 40-over match, in contrast, a side could afford to lose 4 wickets in the first 25 overs and still attain a defensible total. In this first phase it would wish to have reached about 110–4 where, in a 50-over match, it might be 130–4 after 30 overs. Working back, then, from adequate scores 15 overs from the close very much determines the approach suitable for the earlier parts of an innings.

There is not, in practice, a great distinction in this regard between 55- and 60-over matches, but both differ markedly from the Sunday game. In each of the longer forms, if the openers, or an opener and a No. 3, can become 'set' then acceleration will begin during the period perhaps between overs 20 and 28. When Northamptonshire played Nottinghamshire in the NatWest Trophy final of 1987 these tactics went somewhat astray. In a match reduced to 50 overs a side by rain, Northamptonshire still subconsciously played to the long-game tempo, when the loss of only 10 overs had made things much closer to a Sunday contest than simple arithmetic would imply. Thus their batsmen were still defensive to the 'good ball', allowing the bowlers to remain relatively attacking, by the time the 28th over approached. Far from this being the half-way stage, however, little more than 20 overs now remained and acceleration had failed to come soon enough; Northamptonshire's feel for the rhythm of the innings, their sense of when to launch the offensive, had been upset. Caught between Sunday League norms and those of the NatWest Trophy, the side found themselves required to pass from reasonable rates of scoring to overdrive in too short a period.

On a Sunday things will advance apace from about the 10th over onwards. At this juncture, a side will wish to have 30 to 35 runs on the board but no wickets down. The increasing tempo should then carry it to between 90 and 100 at the half-way stage and to a final score of 220 to 240. The usual provisos about the nature of the pitch and the attitude of the sides will always, of course, apply but there is a revealing, not to say disconcerting, extent to which one-day games can indeed be reduced to these statistical sequences.

Since one-day matches place the emphasis on keeping to such rigid tactics, it is perhaps not surprising that Sunday League cricket especially is a game heavily reliant on method. Its two halves are exactly divided between the two sessions, the innings symmetrical and uninterrupted. Frequently, sides of lesser cricketing skill can better maintain the game's essential disciplines through these fixed, 140-minute periods, displaying a better command of the requisite one-day line and length, running well between the wickets and mastering the science of controlled acceleration. The teams which attempt to win by exuberance of stroke-play, or which fail to adhere mechanically to bowling and fielding plans, are consistently beaten by opponents of more modest ability on paper. In recent summers Derbyshire, Lancashire and Nottinghamshire are sides who have consistently finished higher in the Sunday table than in the Championship, while Middlesex and Essex have done less well than their talent would suggest that they might.

This can hardly be offered as an excuse for failure. The Sunday League is no longer a novelty and its financial incentives are considerable. All sides do undoubtedly take the competition seriously – in that they try to win it – but some may still mistake individual effort for team rigour. To accomplish the latter, a team must be both very well ordered and self-effacing enough to accept routine. Precisely because the Sunday League is so much more predictable – even the types of tense finish it produces are predictable – sides which submit most uncomplainingly to its logic will do well. The phrase 'the secret of success' is often used in sport; there are in fact few secrets on a Sunday, its cricket less a matter of assessing how to win than of applying oneself with ungrudging efficiency to a number of tried and tested principles.

Since it is easier for them to devote themselves to a set task over a short period of time, certain types of cricketer have flourished in 40-over cricket. Men like Chris Bullen of Surrey, Colin Wells of Sussex and former Northamptonshire all-rounder Duncan Wild tend to be more effective on Sundays than in orthodox cricket; Bullen, for example, played only two Championship matches in the course of 1989–90 despite being brought into the side regularly at the end of the week. Those who can bat as well as apply themselves to their quota of overs are especially valuable in that they give captains the scope either to include an additional specialist batsman or to have six players between whom to share the overs.

This last asset is often more important than spectators realise. At least one bowler will inevitably take some punishment in a limited-overs game, and so it is of great benefit for a captain to be able to bring a replacement into the action and rest the man whose rhythm has deserted him or whose particular pace is ill-suited to the conditions. Moreover, it is often helpful towards the end of a one-day innings to vary the attack as much as reasonably possible so that the batsmen cannot become accustomed to the pace, length and line of one specific bowler. So it is that the Sunday League, more than the other two one-day competitions, has developed a certain kind of player: the man who can contribute middle- or late-order runs and be relied upon to complete eight economical overs.

The degree to which the bowler strives for something more than containment and positively seeks wickets differs considerably between the types of one-day game. The principle that a couple of quick dismissals are worth a lot more than 20 runs saved through restriction (the more so if a potential match-winner is removed early) perhaps applies universally. On a Sunday, however, wickets are something of a bonus in that 40 overs will rarely provide sufficient scope to bowl a side out, and a team's strategy cannot be geared even minimally to attack for more than the four or five opening overs. Exceptional bowlers who can generate extreme pace off restricted Sunday run-ups, men like Malcolm Marshall or Sylvester Clarke, may perhaps bowl for wickets at all times, but few have the gifts which command this luxury. Even a superb fast bowler like Michael Holding would not ordinarily attack in the Sunday League. One of the more pertinent distinctions of the cup competitions, then, is that a side can continue to seek wickets for far longer periods.

Irrespective of whether they habitually like to set targets or chase them, if a pitch is a little green or damp early on teams will usually insert the opposition in the hope of taking wickets and thus of denying the all-important fluent start. Even without the encouragement of the conditions, a 60-over game might typically commence with a fairly orthodox field containing three or perhaps four close catchers. For such aggression to be sustained, success would have to be almost instant – inside the first five or six overs, say – but two close catchers might well be maintained for some time thereafter. Depending on the surface upon which the match is being played, and thus the rate of scoring attainable, regular breakthroughs in a 55- or 60-over game might well see the search for wickets continue through the first 30 overs. This will be particularly apparent in the pressure applied after a dismissal. Once a Sunday game is under way, it is extremely unlikely that a close catcher will be brought up for an incoming batsman. In the longer match, however, the new batsman will often be met by two slips, even following a relatively productive stand which has contributed to a reasonable start.

Such hostility cannot be pushed too far. Professionals are often criticised for seeking restriction even when their opponents are well placed for victory and they therefore need to take wickets: in other words, 'the best way to stop runs is to get people out'. Yet the censure is rarely valid. If a side is chasing 260 to win and, having scored 170, loses its third wicket with 15 overs remaining, it is clearly the favourite to win. The real debate is not whether the fielding side should seek to save runs *or* take wickets, but over the precise way in which wickets can be taken.

Most captains would not place a close catcher for the new batsman unless they had an exceptional bowler at their command who could both deny the newcomer runs and threaten to produce an edge. The justifiable fear would be that experienced batsmen are now so calculating in their ability to work the ball about the field that any gap created by employing a slip, for example, would be exploited immediately. The more likely response would be for the fielders and bowlers to become yet more alert to the need to save the single, thereby ensuring that the new batsman faces as much of the bowling in the next few overs as possible. A fielding side trusts to its nerve and, as importantly, to the knowledge now confirmed by countless one-day examples that apparently unassailable positions are often in fact surrendered. The hope will be that fifteen minutes of great application at this stage (with 15 runs coming from the next four overs, perhaps) will push up the required run rate to nearly 7 from its present 6 per over, and the pressure thereby exerted on the batsman would be considered more likely to bring another wicket than the overtly dramatic gesture of calling up a slip. Thus what may appear to the onlooker to be mere containment when wicket-taking aggression is required is in fact a more sophisticated version of the same purpose; there is more than one way to skin a cat.

Although it is generally true that one-day matches should take place on ideal, 'batting paradise' pitches, needless to say, this is not always the case. It is very important for both sides in a one-day game to make a rapid and accurate assessment of what, on the evidence of the first phases of the match, should provide a winning score. This will clearly have an influence on the balance between attack and defence which, in the longer matches, the fielding side seeks to strike; it is also a primary determinant of how the batting side approaches its innings. It is vital for the opening batsmen to weigh up the pace and movement of a pitch and thereby calculate its potential yield of runs in the allotted number of overs. If, on a slow, seaming pitch, a side bats as though it envisages making 275 in 60 overs when par is in fact 30 or 40 less, it is far more likely to lose valuable early wickets in overambitious stroke-play. An astute and experienced opening batsman should be able to return to the dressing-room and say, 'This is a 220 pitch', to provide his side with a goal to aim for. At the same time, the best fielding sides will be equally able to interpret conditions and judge whether the opponent's rate of scoring is acceptable or genuinely threatening.

The common argument about whether to chase runs or bat first on winning the toss is, for this reason, often less relevant than is imagined. Pressure does not automatically fall on one side more than the other in a second innings, but rather it derives from the assessments made of what the pitch should be able to offer. If the side batting second is confident that even an ostensibly stiff target is well within its compass, it will take all the more encouragement from having restricted the opposition. Conversely, when the side fielding first knows that as few as perhaps 220 in 60 overs represents excellent batting under the circumstances, it inwardly concedes that the run chase ahead will be hazardous. One-day matches between experienced, professional teams are often won by the side which has bowled the fewer bad or inappropriate deliveries in the conditions. An attack which knows that it has given away 20 or 30 unnecessary runs with, say, ten genuinely poor balls at key times also knows that it has put its batsmen at a psychological disadvantage; they will either have to be similarly aided or play appreciably above themselves to win. In that sense, whether the total is 200 or 300 is not necessarily important.

It may be helpful to conclude this examination of one-day formulae with a note on the unique disparity between Northamptonshire's success in cup competitions and their record on Sundays. On the surface, a side with such batting ability as has taken them to more one-day finals at Lord's in the last fifteen years than any other team might be expected to do well in 40-over cricket. In fact Northamptonshire are historically the poorest of all the seventeen sides in what is now twenty-three summers of the Sunday League. They will typically try to score far too many runs in boundaries, rather than proceeding in a more disciplined way by picking up singles with astute placement and running; the old adage, 'get your singles and the fours will look after themselves', is particularly valid here. In their bowling the side has been guilty of failing to adapt the strike mentality of a weekday to the harsher, more workmanlike requirements of relative containment. Worse still, perhaps, an unconscious downgrading of the Sunday League's credibility in the side's outlook – neatly providing a justification for failure – has prevented the players from acknowledging why their methods are ill-advised. Every time a dressing-room discussion stresses the particular needs of the match ahead, so it is almost the more likely that the batsmen will go out and do the opposite of what they have just agreed is prudent.

There can be no grounds for even perverse pride in this allegiance to inappropriate Championship tactics. Although few players particularly enjoy the Sunday League, it is very dangerous to excuse any failure to work hard at the game. If it is to be offered as serious sport, it should be played as such; unprofessional attitudes of mind on a Sunday afternoon may well reappear elsewhere. A more beneficial response might be to urge a redefinition of the game's status.

Players resent being judged as cricketers by what, technically, are the irrelevant criteria of Sunday performance. Yet at the same time clubs speak of the 40-over game, and present it to the world, as though it were a competition of real cricketing merit. Undoubtedly, the players would be a great deal more comfortable with the Sunday League if they felt that it had been divorced completely in the public mind from the game at other levels; they increasingly express the opinion that Sunday cricket should be marketed differently, that it should be made more evidently a thing apart. This might entail coloured clothing, pre-match entertainment or, indeed, anything else which removed from the occasion its pretence of sporting significance. It has become common to hear people say, 'I like the Sunday game but I don't like the other sort'; yet they do not say, 'I like pro-am golf but I don't like the Open' or 'I like pantomime but I don't like theatre', because they recognise that these are contrived, quite separate entertainments. Cricket would be well served by a similar discrimination.

One-day cricket, then, is a game in which batsmen seek merely to abide by the iron laws of the scoring rate, and bowlers pursue a mechanical observance of the limited theories of containment. Yet surely there is something beyond this; surely there are abilities which give the bowler or fielder a more elevated role than that of punchbag alone?

The successful one-day bowler is often the man who can vary his length and pace to keep the batsmen guessing. It is a level of improvisation whose value is almost certainly restricted to this form of cricket alone in that it is specifically designed to prevent someone scoring 5 or 6 or more runs an over, but not necessarily to take wickets. Essex's John Lever would perhaps be the perfect example here. Able not only to change pace deceptively, he could also assess how well set his opponent was, what were his one-day strengths, and therefore which fields and deliveries might best frustrate him. In short, he was able to implement a different plan to restrict each adversary.

Slow bowlers, too, with their ability both to vary their pace and to force batsmen to pursue them, are also very often the most able to contain. With the exception of the unique slow-medium pace of Kent's Derek Underwood, the slower the bowler, the more effective he is likely to be. Contrary to received wisdom, the bowler who can offer flight and variations of trajectory through the air is better equipped than the man who bowls the standard, flat, one-day line of leg stump to a six/three on-side field. Slow spinners like David Graveney or Vic Marks might concede the odd 6, but they are much less vulnerable to the run down to third man, the slice over cover or the glance wide of short fine-leg, if only because there is no pace on the ball for the batsman to use.

The value attached to variation and tactical adjustment here is appropriate not only to individual bowlers, but to their organisation as a group. Sequences of bowlers who can complement one another in diversity have a particular worth of their own. Northamptonshire's best 40-over seasons in the mid-1980s were not built around the customary Sunday bloc of mean medium-pacers; instead, the side relied heavily on its ability to field three completely contrasting spinners, Nick Cook, Roger Harper and Richard Williams. Thus the attack had at its disposal 24 overs from men of widely differing styles which could be combined and interchanged as the circumstances required, and comparatively few batsmen were able to cope with the constant, unsettling revision of their plans which this demanded.

For once the spectator interest in a Sunday League match was not monopolised by aggressive batting. Williams tossed the ball up in the air but, given his lack of height and the dull Northampton pitch, gained little bounce; Cook angled his left-armers into the batsman's pads from wide of the crease round the wicket; Harper pursued theories of one-day bowling wholly peculiar to himself and only possible for an off-spinner of his staggering fielding ability. A man of 6ft 5in who could achieve unexpected lift, he would concede the cut but place two men behind square on the off side to limit its value. With his speed and agility in the follow-through he would close the subsequent gap towards orthodox cover by his own unaided efforts. Batsmen, confronted by these three operating as a mutually supportive unit, found great difficulty in coming to terms with the fact that the tricks of one-day improvisation, regarded as their own exclusive preserve, were being annexed by the bowlers. On their own pitch, Northamptonshire proved almost unbeatable.

The deployment of the attack, then, is ideally governed by the same wish to disrupt which leads the best bowlers to seek controlled variation. A team wishes to prevent the batsman from prejudging the ball's likely length and direction over extended periods in which they can build up a winning momentum. Yet the Northampton instance of three spinners who could move rapidly through their paces was exceptional. Usually, permutations on a Sunday are much more limited than in the longer cup games because each bowler has only eight overs in his quota and the fixed time available for one innings requires attacks to bowl more than 17 overs an hour whatever the volume of scoring. It is therefore rare to find captains who have the luxury of adapting their tactics to differing situations. Quite the reverse is true, in fact; the disciplined, almost robotic, way of Sunday cricket means that bowling changes are often known in advance and players become used to the exact fields to be set at any given time.

Thus the two main bowlers will divide their allocation in order to start and end the innings with four-over spells. Such is the adroitness of batsmen at the end of an innings, the theory is that whoever is bowling 'at the death' will inevitably concede a lot of runs. With this in mind, the captain seeks the best of both worlds, hoping that his main strike bowlers will both restrict the flurry of late runs and perhaps find an early wicket or two. The weakest of the change bowlers may bowl his allotment in a single stint straight after the opening bowlers, in conjunction first with the fourth bowler, who splits his eight, and then with the fifth bowler, who bowls his overs through.

Thinking in the longer games will be considerably more flexible and is therefore much more difficult to summarise. If a captain has at his disposal world-class bowlers in one-day contexts, men like Malcolm Marshall, Sylvester Clarke, Curtly Ambrose or Joel Garner, he may be inclined to give them three, or even four, separate spells so that they always have a few overs in hand to be used either to apply the brake or to take a crucial wicket. As both innings are split, the first by the lunch interval and the second by tea (usually taken after 25 overs), further opportunities arise to take advantage of the changes in tempo these adjournments produce. A common ploy is to introduce the spinners in advance of lunch to rush through as many overs before the break as possible and reduce the number available for acceleration thereafter. Batsmen are now well aware of this tactic, however, and will accordingly slow the game to their own pace. Intervals also enable teams to consider significant alterations to their strategy. They may review their agreed field settings, decide to use certain bowlers in new roles or, if batting, change their estimate of the scoring rate required. In these ways, the longer one-day games are much more 'realistic'; they require forms of decision-making which are at least similar to thinking in the Championship, and they retain the emphasis both on fluid tactics and on a continual interpretation of the game's pattern.

The notion of positive containment in one-day cricket will most usually prompt a discussion of fielding, and it is useful to inquire whether outstanding ability in this area can ever compensate for deficiencies in bowling and batting. While no side could say at the start of a match that its fielding will enable it to win, quality fielding at its best may quite noticeably save 25 runs which a more average team would concede. This is significant indeed: a 25-run advantage in a match where the final scores may be between 220 and 300 will effectively counterbalance the failure of a No. 6 or 7 batsman. Runs alone, however, are perhaps less relevant than the respect – or, more to the point, the lack of respect – which the batsman is obliged to show to the field. At some stage in a one-day match, pressure will start to play an increasing role. High-quality fielding inhibits the batsman in these circumstances and makes him far more likely to succumb; very poor fielding, in contrast, can fill him with confidence and shift the burden completely.

In the mid-1970s Northamptonshire's side contained a nucleus of highly talented specialist bowlers – Bishan Bedi, Mushtaq Mohammad, Sarfraz Nawaz, John Dye and Bob Cottam – whose diversity especially made for great potency in the knock-out cup competitions. Each, however, was a far from renowned fielder and collectively they might be held to contribute anything up to 30 runs to an opposition innings before it had even commenced. It was Mike Brearley's contention that, given the tendency for the side to invite pressure in this way when defending runs in the closing overs of tight games, it was highly doubtful that it could ever win a one-day competition.

Whatever a side's individual talent, it carries a considerable weight into every match if it is notoriously substandard in the field. On that basis it is not simply a matter of arguing that a certain batsman is likely to score 15 more runs on average than a rival for his place, and that this makes up for his fielding inadequacy; only if his runs could guarantee comfortable wins would this be true. By their nature, however, one-day games make close finishes inevitable, and a side which can pick out weak links in the opposition field enlists the pressure of the moment to its own cause. In contrast, a great fielder can be so intimidating that the batsman will mentally deny himself certain shots because they will bring insufficient runs. It is as if the surrounding field is being tightened about him.

The key positions in the one-day field depend largely on the nature of the attack and of the opposing batsmen. In principle, however, the fastest men with the best throws clearly need to be in boundary positions (deep cover, deep mid-wicket and third man) where speed over the ground and accuracy of return might conceivably reduce six or seven potential 4s to 2s and 3s. Such boundary fielders need not be defensive players alone. There are certain batsmen of the highest quality who draw great strength and satisfaction from scoring 4s, and a team's strategy may deliberately seek to stem these particular runs in the hope that, by frustrating the batsman, they force him to amend his game and thus make himself more vulnerable. It is a theory which has on occasion been applied (with little success!) to Graeme Hick. South Africa's Graeme Pollock, after leaving Eastern Province to play for Transvaal, was once found out by his former colleagues who bowled deliberately outside off stump to him with three men on the boundary at extra cover, cover and backward point. Unable to resist the bait of this outrageously blatant challenge, Pollock surveyed the outfield contemptuously and three balls later attempted a venomous drive which he edged to slip.

Other important fielders are cover and mid-wicket, less for their athleticism than for their intelligent ability to read a batsman's intentions in playing his shot, detecting from his initial movement whether he is about to be aggressive or artful. A good infielder, such as Worcestershire's Phil Neale, Hampshire's Paul Terry and either of Kent's Cowdrey brothers, will anticipate sufficiently early to be ten yards from the batsman by the time he has completed his would-be push for the single. This image of the gifted infielder, eyes fixed on the batsman and shoulders hunched as he advances on the run to stalk the ball, aptly conveys the idea of positive, even attacking containment in the field. There is in this encounter a hint of that psychological intentness which is so essential to the game as a whole and yet sadly so absent from its one-day form. The fielder consciously tries to break the batsman just as, even on a Sunday, the best bowler follows insights of his own and not simply those of a formula.

The game of cricket at Test and Championship level is probably best termed 'authentic' or 'real' cricket rather than 'traditional' cricket, if only because the ways in which such cricket has been played, and more particularly the diverse paths to success it has offered, have never remained static. The heart of the game's attraction, indeed, has been in precisely this evolving breadth of possibility and variation. Thus the objection to the present power of the one-day game in fact owes nothing to a fear of change, but is based on the fear that improvisation and self-expression may themselves be overwhelmed by the new game's narrowness. Repeated protestations to this effect, however, make little difference; the cheers of lucrative one-day crowds drown out most words of disquiet. However sincere the intent behind ensuring that the Championship carries marginally more financial reward than the other competitions, the incentives to one-day success are so substantial that it is difficult to envisage English cricket surviving without them. When club chairmen declare, 'We've got to win something this year', they grant equal validity to the one-day game – in fact, they give more than equal credence: one-day competitions outnumber the Championship by three to one.

When, as in Australia in 1990–91, England's cricketers are vilified in the popular press for their failure in so-called World Series Cricket, priorities are badly astray. This was once a competition whose results were forgotten almost as soon as they had been published. There is no reason why England should not field different elevens at one-day and Test level, wholly different elevens if players' abilities are not suited to both games. This is not at all to endorse the approach of those counties which sign and retain cricketers with a view to the one-day game; there are many players who, while entirely reputable Championship performers, have at the same time one-day skills superior to those of established Test cricketers. Australia have already partially implemented this dual selection policy, with players such as Simon O'Donnell, Mark Waugh and Carl Rackemann brought into one-day sides but omitted from concurrent Test series. Present and former English cricketers who might fall readily into the same category are John Lever, Colin Wells, John Steele, David Bairstow and Geoff Humpage.

The need at the base of English cricket is to impress on players how distinct are the relative merits and requirements of the two games and to convey this distinction to the widest possible audience. Not only separate international selection procedures, but the separation of the competitions would assist this process; that is, the detachment of one-day internationals from a Test series so that they are played by a different set of players away from the context of a Test tour. This would ensure that tour parties are chosen not with half an eye to the one-day matches, but with full concentration on the Test series, which should remain paramount. It would, moreover, avoid the harm which one-day failure can inflict on the initial Test performances of inexperienced players; the greater the technical skills of a promising newcomer, the more criminal it is that he should be subjected to one-day matches early in his international career. Those of a confirmed one-day aptitude might well benefit from the experience, but many will not. In Australia in 1990–91, it was sorrowful to witness a man so naturally correct as Derbyshire's John Morris heaving across the line of the ball like a novice in a one-day international; that he should then be pilloried for this by the English press indicates how misplaced attitudes have become. Better by far that Morris should have prepared himself in the nets and in preliminary games for the Ashes series ahead, removed from inappropriate criticism.

The advantage of this first step towards establishing a long overdue demarcation in the game is that few practical difficulties would impede it. Cricket authorities will, of course, cite the potential expense of the exercise, but as a percentage of the overall outlay on contemporary tours, increases would be limited, not to mention the fact that there are wider costs to the game itself to be considered. The steady infiltration of one-day cricket is not, and should not be seen as, the latest chapter in the history of the game. Its supremacy would mark a decisive break, the end of one sport and the beginning of another.

SEVEN

Man of Cricket

In November 1990 at the memorial service for the great Yorkshire and England batsman Sir Leonard Hutton, the Bishop of Liverpool – who, as the Reverend David Sheppard, opened the batting with Hutton in Tests – made an important observation. Many people, he said, who had never known or even met Sir Leonard, nevertheless felt an acute personal involvement with him. 'This,' he added, 'is one of the bewitching properties of cricket.' It is also, dare one say, one of the game's most persuasive illusions.

The powerful feeling that in watching a player's performance you come to know him, or that he was born with a character destined to disclose itself on the cricket field, is only half-accurate, not least because of the obvious distinction between his public and private faces. When a cricketer displays qualities of grit or courage or intelligence they are indeed both very evident and entirely admirable, and they encourage a sense of identity and involvement. To ask, however, what kind of people are attracted to cricket, and what kind of people they become in its embrace, is to pose more fundamental questions of the professional game itself.

To answer this, one must undoubtedly look to the man. More to the point, one must look to the changing man and to the deep tensions within cricket with which he spends his career in combat. It is a team game played by individuals; it demands a tenacity which is never far from selfishness; it pushes pride and commitment to the edge of insularity and obsession. The professional cricketer's characteristic attitude to the game is revealing: he both loves it and hates it simultaneously.

Cricketers are often proficient at a number of other sports for which they do not feel the same affinity. No other team game grants them so complete a satisfaction in individual performance; they may derive physical pleasure from playing football or rugby, but the enjoyment which comes from doing well in these contexts is not the same. Football is about the group domination of space; cricket is about an individual's encounter with time. There are, of course, many other forms of one-to-one competition. Sports like tennis, badminton or squash involve a very simple, linear development wherein action prompts reaction, itself inviting further reaction, in a short series forever interrupted by the failure of one player to find the appropriate response. Golf, a pastime which many cricketers adopt, engages the individual in a more involved contest with an opponent, the course and himself. Yet even this complexity does not equate to cricket's.

In cricket, exceptionally diverse levels of competition are imposed upon the individual. He plays directly against a single other batsman or bowler, against the pitch and conditions, against himself, against the needs of the game in terms of attack and defence, and against ten other participants in addition to his immediate adversary. He does this both for himself and in relation to the mood and intent of his team. The fact that he can succeed against such massive odds produces accordingly high degrees of satisfaction. Failure, however, is disliked and resented so strongly because it is often felt to betray a fault of character rather than of ability. It is as if he is being found out not as a performer, but as a person. When the game is going well for a cricketer his elation reflects a very rare sense of fulfilment; when it proceeds badly it can seem almost abhorrent because it is so severely accusatory. Yet cricketers are drawn to expose themselves to this examination, even when it is ostensibly an act of near-masochism.

It may be thought that cricket is a more solitary game for the batsman than for the bowler; if this is true it is only marginally so. Even in the sense that the batsman is involved in one-to-eleven conflict, the bowler is clearly not exempt. The removal of one or two opposing batsmen, for example, will not usually be held sufficient; the big test will be of his ability to return again when the game has altered and new, better established batsmen are set at the crease. It is precisely in such circumstances that any earlier satisfaction can be made to feel delusory, and the weight of the imbalance reasserts itself. Middlesex's Mike Selvey began his Test début in 1976 against the West Indies with 3 wickets in his opening twenty deliveries; in the remainder of that and three further innings in the series, he could only double his haul at a cost of 255 runs. When a bowler is unable to take wickets he is just as exposed as a batsman; he, equally, is one against many.

The nature of cricket and, by extension, of the kinds of sensibility for which it will have an appeal, does not in fact suggest other sports. A more expressive analogy would seem to be with a field like mountaineering. Here also a many-sided challenge – involving the elements, the mountain itself and a climber's state of mind – is confronted in isolation. At the same time the individual can usually only express an effective response to this test in the context of a group endeavour which jointly determines success or failure, as a cricketer's performance lacks full significance if his team is defeated.

It is one of the fascinations of cricket that some of the apparently least suitable people to take on this vulnerable process are precisely those who play the game; those of a certain insecurity and sensitivity have sought out the one sport where such traits will be constantly interrogated. That they do so indicates both an urge towards creative expression and an intense pride in performance. This is a notion more central to cricket than is probably recognised: if such pride is lost, or lapses into self-interest, the cricketer will not oblige himself to keep going in circumstances where his natural reaction may be to relax or withdraw. Once pride of performance has been significantly weakened, the pursuit of that unique satisfaction which cricket offers is compromised and, imperceptibly, the game is drained of its purpose.

It is that sense of purpose which lends to cricketers a privilege that few enjoy. A player's creative contribution to a game can be seen to matter, it helps to secure an end; few experience this in everyday life, few are permitted so positive a sense of having determined an outcome. Part of the satisfaction which underpins spectator sport comes from the way in which this element of purpose and significance is transposed into lives which are denied the opportunity to experience it so fully for themselves.

It is hardly surprising that there is often a sense of poignant loss in cricketers after their retirement. The game's history is punctuated by examples of men for whom this deprivation, this absence of creative expression, proved tragically intolerable.

The reasons for seeking a career in cricket in the first place will usually differ from those which assume importance later when the career has been established and a player is attempting to cement his position. Attitudes change as the cricketer tries to deal with the in-built strains and necessary balances of his profession. Just as there is a latent tension in the game between cricket as creative expression and cricket as harsh exposure, so there is an uneasy relationship between individual commitment to team success and preoccupied self-interest.

When a young man enters the Second XI he finds an atmosphere of school-like, even childish, camaraderie; it is a group with far from profound aspirations. As he progresses into the first team he interacts with ever more disparate collections of people and he realises the need to work out his game if he is to survive. Part of the maturity he should then seek lies in the development of a self-reliant philosophy which can enhance both his personal performance and the satisfaction he can draw from it; in short, he needs to ask himself why he is playing the game and what he believes it means. It will be all too easy to avoid this process by hiding within the apparent security of the mob mentality which professional cricket can breed.

A potential professional enjoys his new attachment to the game, its dressing-room banter and the general excitement of a novel world which he has just begun to sample. The life of moving from town to town and staying in well-appointed hotels, for example, is so appealing that he cannot wait for the next away trip. The cricketer gains a very obvious sense of importance; he is engaged in something which people discuss and value, an activity which hundreds of thousands have pursued, but only a handful are able to undertake for reward.

It is when this first attraction wears off that the player realises his one inescapable connection with professional cricket: by definition, it is the field from which he must gain his living. The fact prescribes for him a single-mindedness which is not only indispensable if prolonged success is to be achieved, but is probably the greatest distinction between the keen, hopeful junior and the man who wants to retain a place on the circuit. Once the player is locked into it, county cricket carries the demands of many other competitive professions; it demands real determination and motivation to be as good as, if not better than, those who can take your position. However else these qualities might be described, they can hardly fail to be dangerously close to selfishness, and the player needs to develop an outlook which can ensure that the very effort to secure his fifteen years in the first team does not itself sour and devalue the experience. This awareness of what is needed in a career in cricket, and of the uncertainties which will always be part of it, modifies the man who plays the game; that modification, sadly, can often lead to a lessening of enjoyment and a growing degree of cynicism.

Yet the special satisfaction that comes from success in cricket is never entirely eroded. The player at the age of 30 is not a complete stranger to the emotions he had as a 17-year-old in that the singularity of the game's challenge, and the immense pleasure gained from meeting it, do not wane. It is just as gratifying for a professional to score a century or take 5 wickets in his last season as it was in his first, and it is just as rewarding to contribute significantly to excellent team performances. It is an extremely rare and sad cricketer who has so confused the point of playing that he fails any longer to feel this.

A player's competitive relationship with his team-mates, however, and especially with younger players, begins to mean that satisfaction is accompanied by hints of another emotion: relief that somebody else's challenge has been kept at bay. Any malice in this response is modest in that it would only rarely carry over into happiness at another's failure. But there is an undoubted new edge to success which comes from proving yourself not simply superior to the skills of an opponent, but to those of a team-mate as well.

Social phenomena such as organised sport do not emerge by happy accident from history. The refinement of cricket as a serious, codified game and the first appearance of county sides in the 18th century belong to, and express, the period of economic and intellectual transformation which defined the dominant ideas of modern Western history. Two years after the formation of the MCC in 1787 the French Revolution espoused a philosophical concept of man not as a being bound to the land and its seasons, but as the agent of his own destiny; humanity's ethical foundation did not lie in the appeasement of divinity, but in the assumption of control and self-government. By the 1820s, as cricket was being given an organised structure by the first county clubs, Shelley, Byron and Keats had made subjectivity itself thc fit domain of art.

Individualism, an idea which could unite the alien perspectives of Beethoven and Adam Smith in their common preoccupation with man as the engine of change, found its expression in every sphere. Subsumed within individualism as an important category of modern thought is the secondary but inseparable theme of self-interest. In its classic entrepreneurial 19th-century form, self-interest was embodied in the new towns of the Industrial Revolution from whose blackened factories emerged the definitive modern team game, professional football. Yet it is perhaps the precise relationship of self-interest to individual, creative self-expression which is at the core of the philosophy of cricket.

From an outsider's point of view, cricketers seem to be a far easier group of sportsmen to approach and talk to than others, and as professionals they enjoy a traditional reputation for decency. It is important to be neither sceptical nor unquestioningly sentimental about this image, for both responses fail to grasp the ambiguity of the profession and do a disservice to the game. If cricket is anything it is an activity which rests on the interaction of real people possessing real mental and emotional capacities. There is a danger that the outsider will respond only to the façade, the aura of decent sportsmanship which in some instances will conceal a great deal. There is an equal danger that he will begin to accept the recent portrayals of the modern player as pampered and money-obsessed, a man who flouts the alleged spirit of the game.

Cricketers, in recognising that there is indeed an image to be upheld, do offer an implicit respect to their sport, and they concede, consciously or otherwise, that there is enough in cricket to warrant conversation with those who could not hope to play it professionally. Players may spend most dressing-room time talking about horses, sponsored cars, music and women, but their discourse off the field, even with outsiders, can be unexpectedly serious. There is in this a sense of the demands which the game has placed upon them: most will have to think, not to say agonise, at some length about cricket if they are to play it well. Such introspection can open the way to a readiness, in some at least, to accept discussions which other sportsmen might think themselves better off without.

Were an outsider to come into a dressing-room and spend three days there, however, the abiding emotion he would carry back to the 'real' world would be one of disappointment. There would be much for him to admire, but the high levels of behavioural abnormality to be witnessed would almost certainly leave him disillusioned and even a little sad. Certain aspects of men under stress – tantrums, moodiness, jealousies, aggression or irritating flippancy – are commonly found in dressing-rooms, and such emotions are far more amplified there than in other group contexts.

In a way, it would be unreasonable to expect otherwise. The interrelationship between team-mates is, after all, both involuntary and unceasing and, at one level, rests on constant comparison. There is an almost continuous evaluation of a cricketer's work, and he cannot avoid being measured against the contributions of his fellows. This evaluation takes place in the cricketer's own mind, in that of the spectator, in the captain's assessment and in the club's periodic review of its resources. There is an obvious potential for antagonism in this, an antagonism far more pronounced than in careers which lack such an insistent demand for self-justification. Equally, since players spend much of their time in positions of real pressure where highly-strung emotions are inevitably forced to the fore, it would be quite impossible for these to be wholly left behind on the field.

Part of the responsibility to control these tensions certainly rests with the captain, and his effectiveness will reflect the overall spirit of the club. Nonetheless, much of the burden must fall on the individual cricketer himself; if the team is to succeed he has to recognise this and, where appropriate, repress his own emotions. However, there is a direct psychological conflict here. It is imperative that a side enters a match with real fire and a collective will to do well, but heightened expressions of individual frustration or celebration will detract from the group's ability to share a common bond. One aspect of a player's career is a pursuit of self-fulfilment which places great importance on personal motivation; yet at the same time he must develop a wider grasp of what productive co-operation between people involves. If the one is present without the other, individuality can descend into pettiness and produce a blindness to the worth of another's opinion.

Personal preference here is irrelevant: it does not matter if what one team-mate sees as repellent sullenness in a colleague is to another a glorious disdain. What really matters is the impact of the collection of attitudes and outlooks on the effectiveness of the team and, as importantly, on the creative expression of the individual player. The cricketer who becomes a victim of tunnel vision may or may not be an attractive person to know, but he has certainly made an error of judgement. The more rounded and balanced his development, then the more he can resist petty grievances, thoughts of recent failure and egocentricity, and the more likely he is to do well for himself and his side.

The most level-headed professionals are able to take both success and failure in their stride; their position in the dressing-room, and indeed in the game, is not a matter of damaging torment. They remain true to themselves and know that there are other things in life, and so, interestingly, they gain the most universal respect in cricket. It is not that they avoid the issue by saying, 'It's only a game', or that they lack any pride of performance; but they know why they are playing and what is the place of professional cricket in the scheme of things. It is an attitude which keeps them above envy, selfishness and backbiting.

The daily constraints of English cricket produce their own cycles from which it is not easy to break free. Professionals are not only together for five months at a time, they repeat that intimacy for ten years or more. An individual's character development in that period is interesting to observe. If a young man can make the fullest use of the opportunities which cricket provides – opportunities to meet people, travel, see the ways of the world and gain independence – he can make the gratifying transition into a complete individual. The ability he gains to detach himself from the immediate needs of cricket will be of great benefit to his game.

Too often, however, such awareness arrives late. Rather than developing an objective view of himself and of his team, the cricketer is caught up in the professional round of play, travel, hotels and fast food, and vital chances to explore alternative perspectives from outside this routine are lost. The old school in cricket rightly stresses the importance to the young player of simply talking about the game. Unquestionably, this is a prime element in a professional's education, but it is far too easy to linger on in the cricketing environment. Although the cricketer needs to formulate at some level a philosophy towards his game, this cannot emerge from a consideration of its technical properties alone.

It should not be thought that a professional's almost incestuous devotion to the cycles of the game is the product of mere escapism, a taste for the good life. The company of the fellow players with whom he may spend his free hours might well include the same people he has difficulty with in the dressing-room. The dependency he betrays here is too complex for glib disapproval.

Nor is this lack of a balanced viewpoint always the product of weakness. Nobody was more fanatical about the game than David Steele, and in a perverse way this brought an element of inhibition to his play which prevented him doing full justice to his range. There was a 40-over fixture at Northampton in the late 1970s when the visitors were Glamorgan. Some time before noon, Steele was already on the outfield practising, long in advance of the players' reporting time. By the start of the game over two hours later Majid Khan, Glamorgan's overseas player and, for Pakistan, probably the most unconcerned Test cricketer of the last twenty years, had still not appeared; when he eventually did arrive, he apologised for having driven to the wrong ground. Somewhere between those two extremes, placed side by side in the absurd context of a Sunday afternoon in Northampton, was perhaps the appropriate philosophy of professional cricket.

Steele's outlook was the opposite of the 'mob mentality', but was, in its way, still too restrictive in its grasp of the game. Ironically, the mob mentality itself recognises, at a subconscious level, the shortcomings of the limited view. In their dedication and application to cricket, professionals gather together in their recreation to hide from the possibility that this alone may not be enough. They find safety in numbers to reinforce each other's acceptance of low horizons and to find a means to evade thinking about the wider world. Immersion in this lifestyle provides a guard against the very difficulties of the individual's role in a team game. When a player first comes into cricket his urge to be accepted makes him strive hard to become one of the boys; the problem is to realise the inadequacies of this natural desire early enough and to find the strength and confidence to break out.

Nevertheless, there are many in the game who have managed to pursue a course of their own. Gloucestershire and England wicket-keeper 'Jack' Russell would be cited by most as a cricketer who has not been overwhelmed by the circuit's typical entertainment syndrome and who has found diverse interests; although he is indisputably a cricketer of the highest skill and maturity, it is the spirit of his approach rather than its detail which is important. The pronounced mental freedom from cricket which Russell brings into his life at significant moments is by no means the only route. Graham Gooch's interests, for example, are largely in sport, and much of his thinking is devoted to performance on the field. He will, however, tend to detach himself from the group, and it is not coincidental that it is he and John Emburey, another very strong-minded man, who would argue most keenly for the presence of players' wives on international tours.

An extension of the mob mentality is found in the tendency of many cricketers to become creatures of habit and routine. The same pegs are returned to each year in the dressing-room, the same rituals are performed each morning before play. This is often noted as endearing superstition, but that in itself can betoken a certain narrow-mindedness and insecurity which will reveal itself in play. Although the cricketer must bring a single-mindedness to his play and hones his energies towards an ability to give his all on the field, this process is susceptible to the delusion that anything new will loosen his grasp. Thus there is often a frustrating inflexibility in attitude and opinion, an intolerance of anything which may intrude. What the player might see as maintaining his resolve is in fact the betrayal of his insecurity about himself and his position in the side.

Certain physical and structural supports for these habits of mind can again be identified: professional cricketers spend up to ten hours a day, on two days in three, changed into their playing kit; they cover up to 10,000 miles a summer travelling between grounds; they stay in perhaps twenty different hotels; and there are other elements which are equally constricting. It might be thought, perhaps, that the contemporary emphasis on encouraging patronage and financial support by mixing with sponsors and the occupants of hospitality boxes would broaden the player's horizon; in fact, his public relations duties only serve to reinforce the daily routine and, far from encountering the outside world, he is enmeshed in a further strand of professional cricket's web. At their most ignoble, these social occasions see the player cultivate contacts for possible future benefit and the sponsor usher performing bears into his box. It becomes a relationship of mutual utility, not an act of discovery.

Furthermore, there is renewed stress today on set regimes and the cultivation of a corporate squad identity. Even in training, players run round the boundary en bloc, completing programmes of group exercise. There are widely different views from county staffs on the worth of such practice. Ian Hall, Derbyshire's opening bat and foremost slip fielder in the 1960s, regularly argues that the artificiality of this approach misconstrues completely the nature of cricket's individual demands: the individual player must decide how his mind is best prepared for his own specific task. The concentration required to face the first ball, for example, or to take a catch in the late afternoon, is achieved as the specialist sees fit; extraneous exercise for over an hour before play may only dull a player's attentiveness. Yet the merit of this argument would be disputed by many present players; the increasing drift in county cricket towards an ethic of conformity, however, may well be importing from other team games a standard of 'professionalism' which is not in fact appropriate.

What is misunderstood here, perhaps, is the nature of team spirit, that elusive quality without which it is almost impossible for a side to succeed. Team spirit is not about eleven people going robotically in the same emotional direction; it is all about the player accepting his team-mates as individuals, recognising their faults and strengths, being alert to his own disposition in that context – in effect, controlling his own antisocial leanings and coaxing a similar responsibility from his fellows. In some senses, the greater the diversity, the better the unit can be – always provided that each player is prepared to accept the benefits which the others contribute. It is not asked of players that, although they are always together, each should form a friendship with every other colleague. But players do need to know how to coexist productively, and this is a process which can only be helped by a greater intimacy with, and understanding of, the outside world.

As the last days of the season approach, cricketers begin to affect an almost unanimous indifference: in a car on a motorway four players will 'thank God it's nearly over'. This is so universal that it is either totally sincere or a total front. Every county has one player who daily professes that he hates coming to the ground and every minute thereafter; the truth is that, after six weeks of the autumn, he will be ready to start again. For most players, the off-season means months of doing things which cannot begin to provide the same sense of satisfaction which, if only three or four times, they have gained in the summer. Yet there is bite to their claim; somewhere within it there is a grim conviction.

There is, however, a quite different set of perspectives on the game – those from without. No activity which has a public dimension can only have one unitary meaning which might be revealed from the inside: the ways in which cricket and cricketers are seen and presented must influence what the game and its players become. A consideration of what cricketers believe themselves to be will produce not one, but several versions of their professional identity; they hold a range of self-images which would not be apparent in other occupations which lack cricket's role in the overall system of values and perceptions in society. Thus a player might think of himself as one of many things: the honest craftsman, the would-be national star, the entertainer, the upholder of certain moral precepts, the tortured genius, the toiler et al. All these have a rich significance which goes far beyond the game itself; they reflect the extent to which cricket, as a powerful cultural theme, is made to support varying sets of beliefs and attitudes.

Players are seen by the public against a wider background of understanding, in relation to the public's own habits and categories of interpretation. Players occasionally express astonishment at how little some supporters seem to appreciate the technical and strategic basics of the game they are watching. Although these supporters do not appear to understand the spectacle, still they are drawn back to the boundary day by day, season after season. There is a seasoned campaigner in Northampton's office who often asks why cricket seems to attract those of a certain eccentricity ('odd people'), confessing, with a smile, to fears about her own affection for the game.

At a Championship match there are many types of regular. There are solitary, almost tragic, figures who appear to draw comfort from cricket; slightly disturbed individuals who relate to the game's rituals, its sense of an ordered progression from start of play through lunch and tea to stumps, one innings following another. There are people who respond to the unthreatening nature of a cricket ground and its provision of long periods of escape into another world. Indeed, it is very like another world; with its own divisions of time, its special allocation of functions and its familiar cast of characters, it is akin to the world of a novel or a film. Many of a county's confirmed followers love this appeal of character, this 'bewitching property' in cricket's exposure of individual players to the open gaze. Having watched the same team match after match and seen young men grow into celebrities, they develop unusual depths of sympathy with the individual traits they seem to know so well. These supporters nod knowingly to each other as recognisable characteristics announce themselves once more on the field: impetuousness, diffidence, perseverance, arrogance, susceptibility to pressure.

All are undoubtedly accurate features and significant in themselves, but they do not tell a full tale. The interaction is complex enough to be fascinating but it does not prompt a more unsettling need to explain. For the spectator is seeing only personifications of emotion; what is missed is the three-dimensional picture of personality and the way that the players do or do not relate to each other within the omnipresent team context. The spectator warms, then, to parable or fable, not real life.

The largely generous men and women of county grounds, however, come far closer to the truth of cricket than most. Cricketers are less well served by the surrogate eyes of the media. In matters purely of technical accuracy the professionals discount the quality of witness found in even the serious press, and players who wish to understand what has happened in matches elsewhere confine themselves to scorecards. This widespread scorn for the opinion of all but a handful of paid observers perhaps betrays the same insecure dogmatism discussed above. It is nonetheless based on demonstrable deficiencies: the absence of almost any constructive analysis in the press today and the rarity on national television and radio of commentators who watch anything other than international cricket. However, errors of factual interpretation, even elementary errors, are perhaps not so important as the tone and associations which types of media coverage can impart to the game.

Shortly before her resignation in 1990, in the act of fighting for her political life, Margaret Thatcher chose to employ a cricket metaphor at the core of her Guildhall speech, wrapping herself in the image of an heroic batsman taking on all-comers. There was a certain light-hearted parody in this which acknowledged that the rhetoric was rather outmoded and twee. At the same time the appeal to the aura of cricket was quite deliberate: the imagery of football hardly serves the same ends. Within days it was as if every political rival in her party had sought to reappropriate the sanction of the game for his cause, each ensuring that a reference to cricket appeared in his oratory.

In the minds of those who knew little of the game and cared less for the Tory leadership, however, all these allusions would merely have confirmed an image of cricket as a game of complacent colonels and of the moral values by which their social eminence was upheld: the cricket, in other words, of countless satires. If that version of cricket has become simply comic, new images have crowded in. In the misrepresentations, and even lies, of the popular press there is a continuing desire to reduce a complex game and a complexity of group interaction to the caricatures of soap opera. Players are either good or evil; what can often be an acute expression of skill and character is rendered savagely simple. Cricketers who fail are deemed to have done so due to spinelessness or a wilful contempt for their honour; those who succeed are heroes for the day. That this profoundly conservative cynicism dictates the approach of such newspapers to the world in general is not the point: it is peculiarly inappropriate to cricket and can only abase its meaning.

At the opposite pole to such a redefinition of the game is 'Test Match Special', which presents cricket as something magically untroubling, a game at one with all the consoling myths of English life. Here is the world of cakes and sunshine, jolly umpires and red buses, the world of the suburban nursery and prep school dorm. The fact that millions relate to this as mere entertainment, a diversion from more perplexing realities, does not reduce its potential to formulate cricket's identity. The game is thus contrived into a form unknown to the people playing it.

In the end the question of image influences decisively the tone of what actually takes place on the field and the expectations of the people who watch it. English cricket's desire to sell itself by the pound may have quite unforeseen consequences; the greater the gulf between packaging and product, the more pronounced is the vulnerability to fashion. The TCCB's decision to put broadcasting rights for certain competitions up to tender has committed it in part to the hysterical style of satellite television. Inheriting Channel Nine's delight at revelling in controversy, the image of cricket projected here rests on superficial novelty, manufactured entirely via the screen: so there becomes less and less point in going to the game itself.

In the last analysis, the extent to which cricket remains embedded in the culture depends on a genuine sympathy with its intrinsic qualities. Warts and all, these qualities can only be human. At least, if they cease to be human, there is no longer any meaning to discuss.

EIGHT

First-Innings Score: Twenty Years in the Professional Game
by Geoff Cook

It has always appeared to me a heresy that cricketers should pursue the game professionally for the apparent glory of statistics or financial reward alone. Such aims in no way do justice to a mass recreation which is turned into a paid career for the fortunate few who find themselves contracted to a county. Peter Watts, the brother of my first county captain, Jim, and himself a very talented cricketer who played for Northamptonshire and Nottinghamshire during the 1950s and 1960s, has become established as a businessman of some substance in Cambridge. Throughout my career he was a great help to me in several ways: as advisor, supporter in adversity, technical guide and not least as a personal sponsor, even to the extent of offering employment after my career was over. When Durham's accession to first-class status became a possibility, we had a conversation on the benefits of being a professional cricketer. He argued that, if the career is approached properly, then a cricketer has so great an opportunity to develop as a person, sometimes unconsciously, that he ought to have little problem finding a suitable niche for himself after leaving the playing fraternity.

The complexities of the profession, both personal and otherwise, are manifold. It is the ability to recognise these complexities which, with certain outstanding exceptions, will help the player develop his skills and, indeed, his character. Any person, for example, who is faced with the task of moulding a number of cricketers into a competitive unit will undoubtedly gain management and organisational skills which will serve him outside the game. Any cricketer who seriously recognises the significance of a team or club spirit and consciously works towards its attainment will surely not be a lesser man for his efforts.

As a player gradually begins to accept an accompanying

responsibility through his importance to a club or his seniority, so the process can and should produce admirable qualities. Prime amongst these, perhaps, is unselfishness in the common cause. The ability to assist someone who is becoming a direct threat to your own livelihood is understandably difficult to acquire. As long as it does not entail any softening of the necessary competitive spirit, however, it must be of a certain absolute worth which extends far beyond a cricket field.

In a career that has been as enjoyable, eventful and satisfying as any that could be wished for, there are occasions and periods which present themselves as more memorable than others. Certainly the most traumatic period for me was that following the 'rebel' tour of South Africa in 1982. The history of the tour's organisation and completion has been well documented with my own near-involvement naturally mentioned. My eleventh-hour decision not to take up the contract was a very difficult one to make in the light of both the financial attractions of the tour and the chance it provided to be reunited with so many family friends we had made during previous visits. However, having spoken to several leading cricket figures, Donald Carr (the TCCB secretary) and Ken Turner (Northamptonshire's secretary) among them, I decided not to participate. The reason in the end was very simple: the real dangers to the game, both at national and county level, which the tour posed became clear to me. An international split would have massively jeopardised the future of the county game.

The trauma then began, not in the resulting controversy attracted by the tour and the associated media attention, but in the rifts within the playing staffs of the professional game. Ill feeling and resentment ran free for some time afterwards, with dressing-rooms and clubs developing schisms which time and diplomacy were alone to heal. Northamptonshire was no exception, and this is where my real sadness began. The reasons for my declining the tour were seen as purely selfish by the touring party which included Peter Willey and Wayne Larkins from the county. It was saddening that two players with whom I had shared a dressing-room for twelve years should make that assessment. It resulted in a couple of uncomfortable seasons for the other team members, seasons in which individual motivation became too disparate for the club to progress in one single, healthy direction.

A far more satisfying period had occurred the previous winter and also had South African connections. It was during that winter that I had my first prolonged experience of captaincy when I was appointed to lead Eastern Province through the 1980–81 season. There has been an attempt in this book to explain how positions of seniority and respect are reached in the course of a professional's career. Great satisfaction is gained from attaining these landmarks. Although the respect which sportsmen offer is universal, to achieve a landmark in another country brings deeper satisfaction. Approval is so much more hard won there, and it was a source of high fulfilment to feel that an approach to cricket and cricketers, shaped by ten years within the English county game, could bring such a great honour overseas.

These two illustrations perhaps reflect what cricket is about for me. The meaning of the game and the reasons for playing it do not really belong to bat and ball. At one level, the results gained on the field from a day's, a week's or a whole season's work are, of course, the player's *raison d'être*, and ultimately the game will judge him on these results. Equally relevant, however, is the approach of the player to the team game in which he is involved, and it is this which provides a better reflection of the true cricketer.

Such are quite possibly the sentiments of a man at the end of his playing career, retrospectively seeking a more adequate measure of purpose and value than mere figures on a scorecard. There are, of course, pleasures and attractions of a greater immediacy, the daily delights of playing the game which maintain the participant's enthusiasm. There are those, both inside and outside the game, who are prepared to malign it, but one thing is indisputable: county cricket is the home of many highly talented players, and it has been a source of immense pride that I have been able to witness this talent at close quarters. The supreme skill and excellence which is regularly on display throughout the English summer is sadly too often overlooked or misinterpreted. There is a fascination in watching truly great players – their styles, their means of motivation and their characters – which can be shared by the spectator, but never realised.

Hence, perhaps, the optimism and excitement which is felt in April and permeates pre-season practice each year. If players apply levels of application and commitment to their preparation at this time of year which are not sustained for quite long enough as the season progresses, the blame is not theirs alone. Spectators are probably less able to sympathise here than they are with the more obvious trials of the game, but the retention of early-season playing standards is almost impossible given the volume of commitment a summer demands.

One of the aspects which help sustain the player's full attention is the repeated arrival of important matches. The stimulation provided by such fixtures both before and, if the team has done well, after they have been played is vital; they become a real boost to the adrenalin flow during a heavy season. I looked forward to these matches so positively throughout my career, regardless of the form I was in, that my personal frustration was sharper in their aftermath than in the midst of the grind of more mundane matches. Recalling the keen anticipation which those games produced and contrasting my negative reaction to the playing of Test cricket only exaggerates the sense of unfulfilment with which I associate that phase of my career.

I have attempted to indicate the elements of the game that are important to me, those which have given satisfaction and direction. Defining what cricket has meant to a player professionally involved in it is not a matter of neat formulations, but perhaps I might try to imagine those aspects which will most be missed in my retirement.

The chief aim of any team is to maximise its talents to produce victory; this is the goal and thus victory brings corresponding satisfaction. As cricket is a team game played by individuals, the emotion whose denial I will feel most acutely is the pleasure felt in personally contributing to a successful team effort. The feeling, justified by a substantial innings, that a challenge has been taken up and overcome is one that can rarely be matched in life. Form has been regained or confirmed once more, the game has been good to you and tomorrow can be approached with relish. Modesty must be retained and consideration for one's colleagues preserved, but an inner warmth quietly insists that, however temporarily, cricket is not so formidable after all. Newspapers will be a more attractive proposition in the morning, and there need be little shame in that. Less defensible, perhaps, but undeniably present, is the relief that tomorrow's possible failure can at least be tempered by yesterday's success.

It must be admitted that the laudable ability to enjoy other players' success is not always so forthcoming. Affiliations are struck up for various reasons in cricket; simple friendship, admiration, similarities and opposites of style. I must confess to enjoying the performances of those whom I respect far more than the performances of those whose values do not appear to marry with my own. That said, it is a vital part of a cricketer's education to share the satisfaction of some players at close quarters. He can learn, either directly or indirectly, why and how fulfilment has been achieved and difficulty surmounted. In that sense, cricket's frustrations and accomplishments can reveal not only the workings of your own character, but that of others around you. This may be seen as an opportunity which the game provides or an obligation which it imposes. Either way, few walks of life offer a similar chance.

The last two decades have seen changes of direction within cricket, the course of which it may well now be impossible to alter. The financial dependence on gate receipts, membership fees and local fund-raising has diminished to such a degree that those factors are negligible in any analysis of a club's balance sheet. As is the case with most sports, cricket is now inescapably part of the commercial world, even to the extent of basic cricket decisions being unhealthily influenced by the financial ramifications they are alleged to have. Never are new directions explored without the involvement of the marketing experts, and so never again will cricket be able to develop teams and individuals as once it could. The cricket business is now moulding a new system, changing the clubs and, consequently, producing different types of cricketers.

Every major cricket ground is the scene of some development, usually geared towards a means of creating substantial income; hospitality suites, executive members' rooms and banqueting halls have become as common as boundary boards.

Northamptonshire have been, in many respects, as positive as most counties. Considering the difficulties which it has faced in terms of physical restrictions, it is to its credit that the club has not only developed commercially, but continued to attract players of the highest calibre. Northamptonshire is generally considered a 'small county', and certainly it has a relatively modest cricketing population to call upon. Yet its teams over the majority of the last twenty years have all been respected throughout the game as capable of formidable cricket. Unfortunately for the club and its members, however, inconsistency on the field has been the hallmark of these teams.

The club I joined in 1970 was at a desperately low ebb. There was a very tangible post-Milburn feel to everything as Northamptonshire tried to rebuild a team tragically deprived of its one real character. A dour, unattractive image had been created by a collection of players such as David Steele, Brian Crump, Roger Prideaux, Albert Lightfoot and Peter Lee; all fine cricketers in their own right but collectively men who struggled to enjoy their game. It was at this stage in 1971 that Jim Watts took over as captain. The bleak, heavy-footed, 'another day at the factory' syndrome of the early 1970s clearly had to be unproductive. It was obvious that a preoccupation with cricket as a job and no more, a matter of personal success alone, was not conducive to self-expression. The introverted attitude was repressing a level of genuine ability to such a degree that the team was doing itself a grave injustice. Two prime examples of this were Peter Lee, who moved to Lancashire in 1972 and twice subsequently took 100 wickets in a season; and Peter Willey, whose true excellence only revealed itself in more comfortable surroundings.

Jim Watts brought a clarity of thought and strategy to the squad coupled with a much more positive attitude on the field. Optimism developed not only within particular individuals, but within the club itself, and this was reflected in a ruthless campaign of recruitment which brought five quality players to Northampton – John Dye, Bob Cottam, Bishan Bedi, Sarfraz Nawaz and the opener Roy Virgin. The presence of these cricketers helped bring out the true ability of Mushtaq Mohammad, who had been in the side since 1964, and Northamptonshire began to play quality cricket. Already, however, inconsistency had begun to show itself. Sadly, Jim Watts left without really seeing the job through, and the captaincy passed quickly through Roy Virgin to Mushtaq in 1976.

An alarming contrast followed as Mushtaq's laid-back attitude to captaincy allowed free rein to the many-faceted skills at his disposal. For pure all-round skill no Northamptonshire attack before or since could match Dye, Cottam, Bedi, Sarfraz and Mushtaq himself. It combined three world-class international bowlers with two of the most effective Englishmen to be found in Championship conditions. The skills displayed were so varied, yet so regularly seen, that the side almost began to take for granted that the opposition would be dismissed cheaply; yet such complacency bred bad, unprofessional habits.

Many times it is said of a sportsman that 'with a bit of so-and-so's application, he would have been so much more effective', and the point is perfectly illustrated by the differing approaches of the teams of these two eras. With only a small infusion of the former's more professional approach into the latter, more honours would certainly have been won. Conversely, the earlier team inherited by Watts at the turn of the decade would have been better served by a freer, less inhibited mental outlook.

Although Northamptonshire's first trophy soon followed (the 1976 Gillette Cup), the club recognised the dangers in a team of one age group and, in 1977, reacted quickly and controversially to remove Mushtaq and all of the recruits save Sarfraz from the payroll. Here was an example of a committee being detached enough to see real problems developing and to take instant, if unpopular, action at the right time.

Now 37, Jim Watts returned from retirement in 1978 to bring stability to a staff reeling from committee decisions with which they were not fully able to agree. The club's concern for the future was further evident, however, in the acquisition of the 23-year-old Allan Lamb and the beginning of overdue ground alterations with the construction of a new pavilion. More one-day finals followed, which reflected steadiness rather than penetration in the bowling and a strength in batting which Lamb did much to revitalise.

After an apprenticeship thoroughly served through seven

seasons, this was an interesting time for me to compare the differing methods, approaches and attitudes among the players. A variant of the Northamptonshire style was emerging, certain Championship rules were altered and, in my first season of captaincy in 1981, the historic change to covered pitches took place. It was with the benefit of the experience of these different captaincy and playing styles that I was able to shape the order of priorities for the Northamptonshire of the early 1980s. The strength still lay with the batting: Willey was approaching his best, Lamb was busy proving himself in English cricket, Wayne Larkins, as is still the case, was capable of brilliance and Richard Williams was an aggressive No. 5. The bowling was varied, with a mixture of spin and seam, but lacking consistent penetration and continually frustrated by the inherent slowness of the pitches at Northampton.

My belief was that gambles would often have to be taken to create chances of victory. This suited the county's philosophy that the notion of professionalism should not restrict the players' ability, and indeed responsibility, to provide entertainment of a real kind. I have always abhorred the growing trend towards manufactured results where the end does not justify the means and too often the cricket that is provided insults the spectator for long periods. With a touch more foresight and a willingness to take occasional risks, these situations can be avoided and cricket can be played with a continuous competitive edge. One of the abilities a cricketer must possess is the capacity to enjoy his cricket. As we had seen at Northampton, when this is absent justice is rarely done to ability. It was felt that a positive approach would go a long way towards creating an enjoyable atmosphere.

Such a theory, however, carries certain consequences. If you are positive, you necessarily risk defeat on occasions. It is then very much down to the individual's common sense to accept the reverses and approach the next day as a new challenge. This might be called an 'adult' approach, and the Northamptonshire players were consequently treated as such, with the licence to live, prepare and practise as grown-up individuals. The group approach was felt unwanted and unnecessary, and I believed, naively, that if the players were given reasonable handling off the field then total commitment would follow on the field. Granted an even rub of the green, results would then reflect the team's ability.

Ultimately, this proved too vague and sweeping a philosophy. In retrospect, the team demanded, paradoxically, both greater personal, individual attention and at the same time a more organised, group approach. Instinctive skill and tactical flexibility was gradually replaced by the need for organisation and control; the balance had not been achieved between order and free expression. This I failed to recognise from within, and slowly one of the club's prime assets, its team spirit, began to dissolve with predictable and saddening results.

In much analysis of the game the concept of the correct balance, apparent in so many situations, is paramount. Is there to be physical work or relaxation; routine practice or individual mental preparation; discipline or the more casual approach; the iron hand or the velvet glove? The questions do not end here, but far larger issues loom. To what extent must a group philosophy be consciously expounded and defined rather than allowed to emerge on its own? In practical terms, should this mean that a team talks as a collective every session, every day or every week? Where, in short, does direction end and self-realisation begin?

Somewhere between the extremes which all of these (and many more) dilemmas imply, is a correct balance. Yet it is not even as easy as that. Because county cricket proceeds on such a day-to-day basis, evoking at various stages the whole range of human emotion, this balance can only ever be provisional, shifting with different circumstances. Inflexibility is a dangerous trait in the marathon of an English season.

In this book we have continually raised issues which have a bearing on captaincy. Understanding these issues, although a necessary prelude to good captaincy, is not the same as good captaincy itself. The aim is clear enough: to maximise the sum of abilities which a collection of players is seen to have. Following that line of thought, the player chosen for the task should be the one most likely to strike the required balance: if, in this undertaking, he himself can realise his fullest ability as a leader, the side will have achieved as much as it can.

Nothing more can really be asked. Northamptonshire's Greg Thomas likes to repeat the observation that no single job in professional sport is more difficult than that of the captain of an English county cricket team. For the most part, however, it is more than worth the effort.

NINE

Observing the Form
by Neville Scott

On Easter Sunday 1985 I was in Bhubaneswar, in the East
Indian state of Orissa. The still, pre-monsoon heat was general
and inescapable; the cold water in cheap hotels turned hot
on touching your body. England's cricketers had long since
returned to their homes, where they would confide, no doubt,
those tales of touring privation which they are discouraged from
recounting to cameras. My only contact with their progress,
despite three months in the country, had been via the transis-
tor radios of fellow passengers on interminable, crowded bus
journeys.

Trying to confirm a berth reservation made elsewhere for the
Madras Mail train, I was at Bhubaneswar station both that
Sunday night and the following night. Each time, a thin, mad
woman sat alone on the platform in the dust, singing softly.
Her size and her song and her constant, uncertain smile made
her appear like a young child, but she was probably about 50.
With one arm she held her knees to her body, with the other she
made gestures which begged alms from occasional passers-by.
For about fifteen minutes each night I waited by her, taking
a cold drink before returning to the office where they debated
my difficulty; I listened to her song. Before I left the second
time I looked at her and returned her smile; she grinned even
more, and for a few seconds we laughed with each other. It has
occurred to me since that that was probably the single mark I
left upon India in three months; not the coins I placed in her
hand, but the contact made for a few minutes in the night with
a mad woman by a railway line.

On summer days in England I go to the cricket. There, for a
time, the spectator knows a rare freedom, the freedom to think
for himself, the freedom to create. Events occur before him which
are meaningless until he himself supplies meaning. Not the
mechanics of the piece – a grasp of the rules is a purely technical

proficiency. Instead, it is the place of each element in an overall process which has to be translated, however contingent the interpretation. Nobody can prompt the spectator to the answer they want; nothing can carry him to a predetermined end. The narrative unfolds, and he alone gives it sense.

A Frenchman or an American is truly astounded by only one aspect of cricket – its length. That a single match can last three, or even five, days is utterly outside his experience. Unknowingly his astonishment isolates the essence of the game's separateness. Although comprised of a series of separate, almost frozen, moments, cricket cannot be understood outside the context of time. Indeed, a cricket match is only ever entirely appreciated in retrospect; only then is it clear at what point the initiative decisively shifted or precisely how the draw was determined. Despite this, however, a constant assessment is required of the onlooker as he watches from minute to minute. This is the demanding paradox at the heart of cricket. No other game so enables the spectator to pose questions in advance of the play, to outline those issues upon whose resolution the progress of the match will depend; yet as each question is answered so others arise. Cricket is not observed: it is engaged.

In the last stages of the long descent from the cool, tea-planted slopes of Darjeeling, India, you gaze out at dusk across hillside after hillside of tropical rain forest. The sight is of a beauty which is quite breathtaking. Our response to such beauty is so natural that no further comment seems necessary: when we remark to somebody that a landscape was 'inspiring' or 'magnificent', the point is taken, our enthusiasm understood.

This is in fact misleading. Our apparently natural association of scenery with beauty is both relatively modern and, as a universal cultural theme, very Western. In Shakespearean England, for example, people found something profoundly disturbing in nature; the wilderness was to be avoided as an unknown malevolent tract devoid of the verities of family, village and rural ritual which brought security and purpose to human life. It took affluence and urbanisation, in effect, to change perceptions of uncultivated nature, and Romanticism to invest it with an aura of majesty. When you travel to far-flung regions of the world to see the 'glories' of landscape, the invariable response of those who live there, be they Guatemalan Indians or Filipino tribesmen, is bewilderment. They are entirely friendly and welcoming; it is just that they cannot begin to understand why you have crossed the world to see mountains. The natural environment will certainly have its own meaning and a place in their own cultural scheme, but this will be semi-religious or it may emphasise ancestry and sense of belonging: the mountains are the home of gods or spirits or the community's forefathers. Landscape is something of which the human is a part; it is not something to be surveyed by a detached eye which pronounces it 'beautiful'.

This particular trick of the Western eye is born of an escape from dependence on the soil. When we stand apparently independent of the world about us and view it as an entity separate from ourselves, our interaction with it is aesthetic and even intellectual. The enjoyment of what we see is to a degree an enjoyment of our very ability to engage in that interaction. In the rain forests below Darjeeling, the view is at first sight rather uniform. Only gradually does the eye recognise variation in shades of green and pattern in the contours. The idea of harmony that this appears to convey, a harmony we call beautiful, is the result of our applying our own label, our own significance, to the scene; we have acted creatively, we have interpreted. Another age or another culture would 'see' a quite different significance; or, rather, the landscape would already have a predetermined, received meaning, the meaning ascribed it by the community.

Twenty-four hours down the line from Darjeeling you emerge into the streets of Calcutta. Brazen, strident advertisements mounted on vast hoardings outside the station present the exact opposite of your experience in the hills a day before. They offer brash, unequivocal invitations to the good life for the masses of Bengal; one particular brand of soap or of cigarettes will transport you to the world in the poster. Here you are not asked to interact or interpret; you are enticed, coaxed to submit or obey.

We are everywhere in our lives surrounded by versions of how the world works and of how we ourselves should behave or think. It is not only the approved lifestyles promoted by advertisers or the self-serving half-truths of politics. There is a tone in popular television which bids us be reconciled, to embrace the myth of universal happy endings; there is a gleeful, almost childish, pretence in bright lights, magazine gloss and wholesome shop windows that the world is clean and clear. Such is our present lot: the façade has become the reality.

Literary theory over the last fifteen years has imported heavily from France. Two concepts in particular speak of 'writerly' and 'readerly' fiction; they appear cumbersome in English translation but draw quite a simple distinction. The 'readerly' text, be it a novel, a play or whatever, is what we might call 'easy to read' or 'very readable'. It carries the reader on an untroubled path, presenting a rounded world which is easy to grasp; it flows fluently from beginning to end. As such, the argument goes, it distorts the truth and is only able to move so smoothly because it accepts one or other of the prevailing myths of its age. The 'writerly' text, in contrast, is often what in Britain is called 'difficult'. It refuses the illusion of comfortable progression and constantly disrupts our easy relationship with the narrative; it forces the reader to confront things from different perspectives.

Thus although Dickens leads us through the evils of Victorian England he brings his story, without great disquiet, to a calm conclusion; all problems have been resolved, all loose strands have been comfortingly tied. A frequent Dickensian device is the invention of a philanthropist who conveniently solves outstanding hardship. Thomas Hardy, in contrast, upsets the progress of his tale not only with shifts in time and location, but by allowing different and conflicting themes to intersect and clash. The mature Hardy novel moves not to completion and security, but open-endedness and tragedy.

It is certainly not appropriate to claim for cricket the tragic qualities of a Hardy novel; nor, indeed, could it very readily be argued that in its ever-changing fortunes alone a cricket match undermines prevailing myths. If cricket can be compared to drama, then by preserving the illusion that, despite all the switches and complications of its plot, a finite conclusion will be reached it comes closest to comic structure, not to that of tragedy.

The analogy of the 'writerly' text elaborates a much more

modest argument. At a cricket match, the engagement of the spectator with the unfolding narrative he is attempting to follow is not an easy one; he is not simply carried along on a fixed flow of consequences. His relationship to the piece is complex, hearteningly so in fact. Like the relationship between the eye and the landscape which it sees as beautiful, it is deeply interpretative. He is not force-fed his conclusions, as so often he is in life. Cricket, in requiring its spectators to think for themselves, shows them rather more respect.

The game does, of course, have its conventions, those recurring themes and patterns which sometimes enable you to recognise the kind of match which is emerging. As in literature, such prior knowledge is often most useful when convention is unexpectedly confounded. And yet the more a match abides by known patterns, the more intensely a spectator will feel that the game has been cheated of its essence. When a Championship fixture is played on a pitch so good that each side is almost guaranteed a high total, cricket is not simply boring, it has descended into parody; it has become self-evident, 'readerly' indeed. Interestingly, when Geoff Cook looked for a metaphor to convey the difference between one-day and authentic cricket, he contrasted the appeal of a whodunnit with that of a novel. With one-day cricket, once a novelty but now a full-scale incursion, the world of the façade closes in.

Something has been absent in this assessment. If cricket spectating involves an order of participation more usually associated with the theatre than with a game, there is this difference. The actors we watch in a cricket match are not speaking lines; they are realising the possibilities of their performance even as they enact it. Upon their ability to forge a path to completion, and to fulfil the demands which this route will make, rest the hope of reaching their own conclusion. Cricket is not a puzzle, an anagram got up for our diversion. Its permutations arise from the activities of human beings, not the play of statistics; of human beings striving over days to impose their pattern on a sequence of events. This they do in full view, quite unable to conceal their humanity. They are not acting their characters, they are exposing them; and we can look on.

We do not see everything, of course. Most crucially, perhaps, we see only individuals; we do not know of the interaction between those individuals nor, indeed, do we have any right to. What we so often do witness, however, are people trying to overcome challenges which are as clear to the spectator as they are to the player. There is, on these occasions, an extraordinary sympathy of identification, more intense by far in cricket than in any other sport. Everybody recognises what has to be done, and each player is known to be capable, in terms of ability, of meeting his requirement. What will follow, then, is an examination not of talent, but of personality, and it can be an examination almost as exhausting to behold as it is to endure. In these situations we are, in truth, scrutinising people, not deeds; it is almost as if we are presuming to intrude where we should not dare.

It used to be claimed that 'the game's the thing', that winning does not matter. Few who have ever played would endorse that empty rhetoric. But for a certain kind of spectator, which team has won is invariably less important; it is the experience of engaging the game which stays with you, of being party to a creative act. So fleetingly is the spectator ever allowed to realise this capacity in his own real life; so limited is his intimacy with the self-expression of people seeking control over their own destinies. Cricket gives a glimpse of what is everywhere else denied.

When I was a child I listened to a radio interviewer asking John Arlott what was the most important thing in his life. To her dismay and my discomfort, he placed cricket far in the background, out with the also-rans. Other things – the persistent fact of a mad woman on a station in India, for example – are infinitely more significant. But there are more discreditable ways of consuming a summer day in England, surer ways of resigning your humanity. If it is an escape, it is perhaps an escape worthy of us. For, essentially, we *cannot* know of cricket if we only cricket know.